T0245961

Public Catastrophes, Private Losses

The Feminist Bookshelf: Ideas for the 21st Century
A project of the Institute for Research on Women at
Rutgers University

The Perils of Populism
Feeling Democracy: Emotional Politics in the New Millennium
Public Catastrophes, Private Losses

Public Catastrophes, Private Losses

EDITED BY SARAH TOBIAS
AND ARLENE STEIN

Rutgers University Press

New Brunswick, Camden, and Newark, New Jersey

London and Oxford

Rutgers University Press is a department of Rutgers, The State University of New Jersey, one of the leading public research universities in the nation. By publishing worldwide, it furthers the University's mission of dedication to excellence in teaching, scholarship, research, and clinical care.

Library of Congress Cataloging-in-Publication Data
Names: Tobias, Sarah, 1963- editor. | Stein, Arlene, editor.
Title: Public catastrophes, private losses / edited by Sarah Tobias and Arlene Stein.
Description: New Brunswick, NJ : Rutgers University Press, [2025] | Series: The feminist bookshelf : ideas for the 21st century | Includes bibliographical references and index.
Identifiers: LCCN 2024016308 | ISBN 9781978838758 (paperback) | ISBN 9781978838765 (hardcover) | ISBN 9781978838772 (epub) | ISBN 9781978838789 (pdf)
Subjects: LCSH: Crises—Social aspects. | Feminist theory. | Climatic changes—Social aspects. | Feminism and racism. | Drug control—Social aspects. | Pandemics—Social aspects. | Covid-19 Pandemic, 2020—Social aspects.
Classification: LCC HN18.3 .P84 2025 | DDC 363.7—dc23/eng/20241009
LC record available at https://lccn.loc.gov/2024016308

A British Cataloging-in-Publication record for this book is available from the British Library.

References to internet websites (URLs) were accurate at the time of writing. Neither the author nor Rutgers University Press is responsible for URLs that may have expired or changed since the manuscript was prepared.

♾ The paper used in this publication meets the requirements of the American National Standard for Information Sciences—Permanence of Paper for Printed Library Materials, ANSI Z39.48-1992.
rutgersuniversitypress.org

To the memory of Carmen Vázquez

Contents

Public Catastrophes, Private Losses

Introduction

SARAH TOBIAS AND ARLENE STEIN

Just as we were finalizing this volume, the skies over New York City turned a jaundiced yellow, then orange, and the air began to smell like burning metal. The cause: Canadian wildfire smoke seeping into the United States, snubbing territorial borders. Journalists described the "apocalyptic fog" in the Northeast as a "hellscape" and an "eerie" portent of things to come (France 24, 2023). A few hours before New York's air quality index reached the "very unhealthy" threshold of 200, one of us received a group text from a friend in the city. "NEED HELP—kinda URGENTLY," she wrote. "Does anyone have an air purifier you can lend me . . . the air is really affecting my lungs." The friend has asthma. She was finding it hard to breathe.

This is a book about catastrophe and how it impacts our individual and collective lives. Catastrophe is defined as a calamitous fate, or a disaster, as something which is unanticipated, abrupt, and often shocking and violent (OED, n.d.). Because they are often unexpected, catastrophes call into question our everyday assumptions of order, predictability, and continuity.

Events, such as wars or disasters, are certainly catastrophic for vulnerable populations. But what of the slower-moving but nonetheless traumatizing effects of persistent degradation, violence, and dispossession? Though less perceptibly shocking than a rupturing event, structural violence and immiseration are also catastrophic. As sociologists note, collective trauma is often the product of a "constellation of life experiences" as well as "a discrete happening." It can be the result of "a persisting condition as well as an acute event" (Erikson 1995, 185).

Sudden, overwhelming events, such as the eruption of a giant volcano or earthquake, are not necessarily catastrophes—even if they quite literally shake things up. To be catastrophic, events or processes (and many catastrophes are processes, rather than discrete events) must cause major harm to people, animals, or ecosystems in ways that are measurable in terms of scope and impact. *Scope* identifies whether a single entity, a group, or a nation, ecosystem, or the global community is injured. *Impact* describes the severity of the injury. How disruptive is it? Does it have short, middling, or long-term effects? Does it traumatize, create fissures between past and present, deny a viable future? Since harms or injuries are invariably dependent on interpretation, catastrophes are not objective "thing[s] in themselves," or even "natural" phenomena. Instead, they are subjective, contextually specific, and frequently fashioned by human behavior (Remes and Horowitz 2021, 1–2).

Our understanding of catastrophe derives from a number of different literatures. In the second half of the twentieth century, observers such as psychoanalyst Robert Lifton (1971) studied the ways the Holocaust, Hiroshima, and other defining events of the twentieth century impacted individuals and communities. Lifton traveled to Hiroshima to study "atom bombed children." In addition to the extraordinary physical devastation caused by catastrophic events such as these, he found that they impacted survivors' sense of themselves—their memory, their biographic continuity, their trust in others.

The psychosocial perspective on trauma pioneered by Lifton and others suggests that in order to heal, survivors must join together with those who are similarly affected and try to rebuild shattered relationships. Sociologists studying the impact of natural disasters, such as floods, have come to similar conclusions. Communities are like organisms, according to Kai Erikson. Disasters exacerbate existing community divisions, destroying a sense of trust, reciprocity, and history that holds communities together. They threaten social bonds and "often seem to force open whatever fault lines once ran silently through the structure of the larger community" (1995, 185). But they can also give rise to new communities—for example, among war veterans, disaster victims, people with AIDS, and others.

In the twenty-first century, scholars working in critical disaster studies have argued that disasters, or catastrophes, are invariably "socially produced" and inequitable in impact (Bonilla 2020; Catlin 2022). Indeed, "their effects are experienced differentially through pre-existing hierarchies of race, class, and gender," a set of stratifications which themselves are politically created and sustained (Bonilla 2020; Remes and Horowitz 2021, 3). Some scholars frame disasters as "the outcome of long processes of slow, structural violence" (Bonilla 2020). Unlike violence that is "immediate in time, explosive and spectacular in space," or that provokes "instant sensational visibility," they argue that "slow violence" suffers from relative invisibility, which complicates efforts to challenge or remediate it (Nixon 2011, 2). Without the existence of "arresting stories" to depict slow violence's toll, it is too easy for policymakers to ignore it (3). This is particularly the case because such violence tends to disproportionately impact women, people of color, and sexual and gender minorities.

This volume focuses on three broad types of catastrophes which are particularly salient today: epidemics/pandemics, anti-Black racism, and climate breakdown. As feminists, we are particularly interested in the ways the public and the private are intertwined, and how, during catastrophes, families and communities become repositories for loss, silence, mourning, witnessing, reconstruction, and reparation.

As the recent and continuing viral spread of COVID-19 and HIV/AIDS demonstrates, epidemics and pandemics create myriad opportunities for mass death that transcend national borders, placing excessive burdens on those inhabiting society's margins. Like a deadly virus, slavery once traversed continents with fatal consequences. Today, especially in the United States, anti-Black racism remains a conduit for death, frequently abetted by racial capitalism and other vectors of structural dispossession. "Let me be clear—every single day people are dying, not able to take another breath," Black Lives Matter co-founder Patrisse Cullors said after twenty-eight-year-old Sandra Bland, a Black woman, died in police custody three days after a traffic stop in 2015 (quoted in Smith 2015). Finally, we confront the possibility of mass death—of humans, animals, and ecosystems—on an unimaginable scale due to shifts in global climate. "Perhaps the term could be *omnicide*. The killing of all," speculates political philosopher Danielle Celermajer (2021). "Not just all humans, as if humans were the only beings that could be murdered" (184–185).

Because government action, or inaction, profoundly shapes each of these types of catastrophe, we refer to them as *public* catastrophes. Together, they demonstrate not only the complex nature of catastrophe and its intersectional effects, but also the way in which institutions of social control create, exacerbate, or alleviate pre-existing harms, inequities, and vulnerabilities. Ben Perkins describes how institutions of social control "have an interest in calling our attention to violence that occurs in dramatic spasms . . . and [asserting] that the violence ceases when the spasm no longer holds our interest. This is how they reassure us that they have the situation under control" (2022, 566). He suggests that fast violence may persist as slow violence, which is equally or more malevolent, if no longer hypervisible. As Christian and Dowler astutely observe, "slow forms of violence imbricate with the fast, and the fast inescapably shapes the slow" (2019, 1072). The same may be said of "slow" and "fast" catastrophe. There is no invisible hand where catastrophe is concerned. Social institutions shape both fast and slow catastrophe and the nexus between them.

Feminists have often challenged the public/private dichotomy, noting that politics, the defining characteristic of the public realm, also shapes the private, and that power relations are ubiquitous. As the essays in this volume make clear, it is impossible to fully understand—or challenge—the harms associated with public catastrophe without appreciating their personal dimension or reckoning with the way power thoroughly conditions our experiences as individuals and as members of communities. Indeed, power also shapes how societies respond to catastrophes and how they are remembered long afterward.

Feminists have often written about the ways in which privatized, slow violence intensifies during public catastrophes. Witness the increase in both domestic violence and child abuse during the COVID-19 lockdown. Feminists have also decried how privatized harms become dissociated from their causes, leaving "victims . . . responsible for managing the harm inflicted on their bodies" (Christian and Dowler 2019, 1069)—a type of neglect (or government negligence) that people with long COVID experience today. Christian and Dowler argue that this type of thinking "works to reinscribe binary divisions of public/private, intimate/global, and active/passive, and the subsequent invisibility of slow violence is shaped as much by these gendered bifurcations as it is by time" (1069). To resist these false binaries and the erasure of slow violence, they argue in favor of considering "fast/slow violence as a single complex" (1070–1071). We adopt this approach too, using the unmodified term "catastrophe" as a signifier for events or processes that cause an exceptional degree of harm on a vast scale, whether meted out in ways that are slow or fast.

———————

The Canadian wildfires, which at the time of writing have scorched over 25 million acres of land and are still not fully under control—are only one manifestation of recent dramatic shifts in the global climate. Between 2019 and 2020, bushfires in Australia claimed over 46 million acres (Center for Disaster Philanthropy 2020). Fires in California burned about 16 million acres in 2020 and 2021 (CalFire 2020, 2021). Amazon rainforest fires cost Bolivia 14.8 million acres in 2019 (Sierra Praeli 2022). In each instance, people have been killed, homes destroyed, lives uprooted. Almost 3 billion animals were killed or lost their habitats in the Australian bushfires (Readfearn and Morton 2020). Meanwhile, intensifying heat is making sections of the world unbearable, if not uninhabitable. Journalist Patrick Wintour (2021) notes that "The Middle East is warming at twice the rate of the rest of the world." He warns that "by the end of the century, if the more dire predictions prove true," large parts of that region will "resemble the desert in Ethiopia's Afar, a vast expanse with no permanent human settlement." The year 2022 also saw devastating floods in Nigeria, Chad, Sudan, Bangladesh, and South Africa, with the prospect of more on the horizon as ice caps melt and seas rise. "It is not quite Apocalypse Now," says Wintour, "but Apocalypse Foreseeably Soon."

One of the hallmarks of such "fast catastrophes" is that they are shocking. Our vocabulary for making sense of the impact of these events often comes from the field of psychology, and the language of trauma. *Trauma* literally means an injury to the psyche caused by a terrifying and disruptive event. It has become a general way we speak about the long-term impacts of these incidents. "To be traumatized," writes literary critic Cathy Caruth, "is precisely to be possessed by an image or event." The traumatized "carry an impossible history within them" (1995, 4–5). Traumatic histories create a crisis in meaning and identity for the groups that survive them (Stein 2014). The paradox of trauma is that it imprints itself on people's lives but makes communicating with others about one's experiences very challenging.

While scholars and activists have written about the emotional resonance of climate change for more than thirty years (McKibben 1989; Mortimer-Sandilands 2010), a new vocabulary has emerged to help us speak about climate trauma. Craps (2020) identifies five different terms in this lexicon. These range from Abrecht's "solastalgia," which implies "the loss of comfort, or 'solace,' when one's home is transformed by external forces . . . mostly or completely beyond one's control" to Cunsolo and Ellis's "ecological grief," which describes "the grief felt in relation to experienced or anticipated ecological losses, including the loss of species, ecosystems and meaningful landscapes" (276–277). Other terms that express our distress at the encroaching climate catastrophe include "ecosickness" (Houser), which conveys concern over the relationship between environmental shifts and pathogenic illnesses in humans, and "Anthropocene disorder" (Clark), which names "a psychological affliction that emerges from the realization of a destructive incongruity between the human scale of daily life and the vast spatio-temporal scales of the Anthropocene" (277). Finally, the concept of "pretraumatic stress disorder" (Kaplan), describes how we "live in fear of a catastrophic future marked by environmental crisis," a condition that may be as anxiety provoking and immobilizing as post-traumatic stress disorder (279).

Despite this emergent vocabulary, Craps argues that "the very idea of ecological mourning meets with strong resistance in some quarters" (2023, 69). This, he claims, is because we have a tendency toward "implicitly treating the planet and non-human beings as inanimate matter," as objects that are not worthy of our grief (70). Verlie (2022) argues that we resist mourning the climate catastrophe because we understand it through a scientific lens. This leads us to detach from it and disregard the distress of those already grieving. She advocates for centering "human feelings as potent apparatuses for knowing climate" (2). Yet arguably, our reluctance to feel loss in relation to the climate catastrophe has less to do with scientific framing, or the dismissal of affect, than with our relative positionality. Experts in the Global North dominate discussions of climate change. As feminist geographer Farhana Sultana notes, these experts often ignore the voices of people from the Global South who are already "feeling, embodying, and experiencing the heaviness of climate coloniality" (2022, 10).

"Climate change is an emergency for everyone, everywhere," the United Nations refugee agency proclaims (Grandi 2021). The seeping smoke and the rising seas lace us together and suggest that our futures, to the extent that they exist at all, are intertwined. They are, of course. Yet at the same time, the climate catastrophe is not an emergency that affects all of us equally. People who live in poverty, women, children, inhabitants of the Global South, and people of color bear disproportionate burdens in relation to the climate catastrophe. The Global North accounts for 92 percent of the world's carbon dioxide emissions (Hickel 2020). Meanwhile, the continent of Africa is only minimally responsible for carbon emissions but acutely vulnerable to the climate emergency (United Nations Environment Program n.d.). Indeed, the Global South, particularly cities in Africa and Asia, faces dire risks from intensified heat and flooding (O'Sullivan 2022). As Ugandan activist Vanessa Nakate puts it, "The Global South is not on the front page, but it is on the front line" (quoted in Campbell 2021).

Because climate catastrophe is linked to colonialism and racial capitalism, climate solutions must foster social and racial justice. "Climate justice fundamentally is about paying attention to how climate change impacts people differently, unevenly, and disproportionately, as well as redressing the resultant injustices in fair and equitable ways," writes Sultana. "The goals are to reduce marginalization, exploitation, and oppression, and enhance equity and justice" (2021, 118). Advancing climate justice entails telling stories that transmit the weight of climate grief borne by inhabitants of the Global South. "If we do not tell the stories of those affected the most, how will we get justice and solutions for them?" Nakate asks (quoted in Campbell 2021). Or, as Sultana puts it, "Without pathologizing or objectifying those enduring climate coloniality, we need to be able to hear and heed their suffering, learn from the embodied emotional geographies of climate, while also registering and celebrating a multiplicity of local voices, stories, ideas, cosmologies, [and] strengths" (2022, 10).

———

Closer to home, the climate emergency is likely to compound pre-existing environmental injustices. In the past decade, authorities in Flint, Michigan, and Newark, New Jersey detected dangerous quantities of lead in city water. In Flint, the immediate cause was a policy decision to supply the city with water from the notoriously polluted Flint River. In Newark, lead pipes transported water to schools and homes. In both cases, structural racism played a central role. Flint and Newark are disproportionately under-resourced industrial cities inhabited primarily by people of color, many of whom live below the poverty line (Almasy and Ly 2017; Fedinick et al. 2019). Neither city enjoyed the same degree of protection from environmental hazards as that provided to other communities. Scientists agree that the climate emergency will intensify the likelihood of pollutants entering the water supply in other similarly under-resourced cities in the future (Hill 2021). To respond with any degree of adequacy therefore requires "a rich understanding of the histories and lineages of the deep incorporation of racism and environmental exploitation" (Tuana 2019, 1).

Indeed, the entrenched legacies of slavery in America meet the definition of catastrophe—of being profoundly harmful and widespread in scope—and in this volume we treat anti-Black racism as such. One of the most pronounced manifestations of slavery's legacy is mass incarceration. Sawyer and Wagner note that the United States has "the highest incarceration rate in the world," with "1.9 million people locked up . . . on any given day." They write that "Black Americans . . . make up 38% of the incarcerated population despite representing only 12% of U.S. residents" (2023). A 2021 report from the Sentencing Project notes that "Black Americans are incarcerated in state prisons at nearly 5 times the rate of white Americans," and that "in 12 states, more than half the prison population is Black: Alabama, Delaware, Georgia, Illinois, Louisiana, Maryland, Michigan, Mississippi, New Jersey, North Carolina, South Carolina, and

Virginia" (Nellis 2021). Yet prison is only one component of the gargantuan system of mass incarceration in the United States. Black Americans also constitute almost 30 percent of about 2.9 million people on probation and about 800,000 people on parole (Wang 2023).

In addition to being subject to excessive rates of incarceration, Black Americans are disproportionately killed by the police. Black Americans have been killed by police while watching television at home, after burning hamburgers and leaving their front door open for air, and even when sleeping in their own beds. Traffic stops have been particularly lethal for Black Americans. "The unarmed, slain black bodies in public spaces turn grief into our everyday feeling that something is wrong everywhere and all the time, even if locally things appear normal," writes poet Claudia Rankine. "Having coffee, walking the dog, reading the paper, taking the elevator to the office, dropping the kids off at school: All of this good life is surrounded by the ambient feeling that at any given moment, a black person is being killed in the street or in his home by the armed hatred of a fellow American" (2015).

The ongoing violence against Black Americans at the hands of the state resoundingly demonstrates that it is wrong to equate all catastrophes with singular events. "While crisis may be an affectively loaded designation of an exceptional temporality, it hinges upon a misrecognition of a crisis-event as a singular, troubling punctuation in a fantasy of an otherwise orderly and undisturbed warp and weft of daily life," Danylevich and Patsavas write. "Such fantastical and distinct temporalities of crisis and normalcy are emblematic of, and indeed foundational to, the control and violence inherent in the logic that organizes racial capitalism" (2021). For Black Americans, the crisis of anti-Black racism is both very old and seemingly endless. As Nicole R. Fleetwood observes, "At every turn throughout our entire existence on this continent, the state and white power have tried to subjugate and exploit us largely by separating us from who and what we love" (2020).

The persistence of state-sanctioned violence against Black Americans has pushed the Black Lives Matter movement to focus deliberately on exposing violence against people of color, especially women, sexual or gender minorities, or people with disabilities, in the hope of ultimately forging a new social contract that values Black life (M4BL 2020). In bringing visibility to Black life and death, Black Lives Matter follows the precedent set by Mamie Till Mobley, whose son, Emmett Till, was lynched by white men in Mississippi in 1955. Till Mobley opted to display her son's maimed body in an open casket. "'Let the people see what I see,' she said, adding, 'I believe that the whole United States is mourning with me'" (quoted in Rankine 2015). Through the political act of making her private grief public, Till Mobley is credited with inspiring the Civil Rights Movement (Farr 2022). According to journalism professor Allisa V. Richardson, Till Mobley's decision to display her son in an open casket began a tradition of "black witnessing" that continues to this day, when Black Americans use smartphones to record police brutality against them and post their videos on social media. But whereas images of Emett Till's body entailed "witnessing through the media," now the mainstream media is itself witnessing content that Black Americans produce (Richardson 2017, 11).

The ongoing violence against Black Americans results in a collapse of time, a blurring of history and the present, the persistence of what Saidiya Hartman calls "the interminable grief engendered by slavery and its aftermath." "How might we understand mourning, when the event has yet to end?" she asks. "Can one mourn what has yet ceased happening?" (2002, 758). The continuing loss of Black lives, and the stubborn refusal of many white Americans to recognize that such lives matter, recalls Judith Butler's questions: "Who counts as human? Whose lives count as lives? . . . What *makes for a grievable life*?" Butler maintains that "loss and vulnerability seem to follow from our being socially constituted bodies" (2004, 20). In this context, some lives are considered worthy of attention, while others are consigned to "the dustbin of the unmournable or the ungrievable" (quoted in Gessen 2020).

———

The social structuring of worth and its relationship to grievability became acutely palpable during the COVID-19 pandemic in the United States. In early 2020, those who society regarded as "disposable" before the pandemic, people whose lives were "shaped by pre-existing inequalities rooted in citizenship status, race, class, gender, sexuality," began "falling ill and dying in disproportionate numbers" (Hooker, quoted in McIvor et al. 2021, 174).[1] Political theorist Juliet Hooker notes that structural racism helps explain the vulnerability of African Americans to COVID-19. This is partly because of the "higher incidences of poverty, [and] environmental racism that leads to more toxic environments in minority neighborhoods, lower rates of access to health insurance, and racial bias in medical care" (175). It is also because Black Americans, and other people of color, constituted a greater proportion of those housed unsafely in prisons and jails, as well as those serving as "essential workers"—nurses, janitors, factory and supermarket workers. Essential workers were both most exposed to the ravages of the virus and more likely to work in jobs that did not provide health insurance.

When a white police officer murdered George Floyd, an African American man, in the pandemic summer of 2020, the nation erupted in protest, and we witnessed what Michelle Commander calls "a collective politics of refusal" by African Americans. Such a politics involves "assuming defiant postures in the imminence . . . of death" (see chapter 2 of this volume). For anthropologist Maya J. Berry, the public mourning undertaken in summer 2020 is a type of "wake work" (as coined by Christina Sharpe) or "consciousness [that] does not engender a state of paralysis but calls upon us to do something" (Berry 2021, 932; Sharpe 2016). Among wake work's imperatives are to pay "vigilant attendance" to premature death as well as "to the intersecting ties that bind us to pathogenic systems constraining the potential for other forms of life and relationality across difference" (Berry 2021, 932). When the Black Lives Matter movement insists that we "Say Their Names" to remember African Americans who have been victims of police violence, they are challenging Black erasure through a type of "vigilant attendance."

This politics of mourning is reminiscent of the ways activists fought erasure in the early days of the AIDS epidemic in the 1980s. Sara Ahmed argues that the "politicization of [queer] grief was crucial to the activism around AIDS and the transformation of mourning into militancy," particularly because it was so easy for *queer* to be "read as a form of 'non-life'" (2004, 156). Acts of public mourning, such as "die-ins," and of collective commemoration, such as the AIDS memorial quilt, vividly brought grief into public view.[2] Activists upended dichotomies "between public and private as well as between affective and political" and simultaneously created "networks of friendship, camaraderie, and community built on a queer archive of testimony, struggle, survival, and response to trauma" (Athansiou 2006, 42).

The approaches to mourning and erasure employed by both Black Lives Matter and AIDS activists are important manifestations of how the personal is political. They also reveal the generative potential of processing personal grief in a public context. Sophia Longo astutely notes:

> By mobilizing grief publicly and politically, the terms of loss and its aftermath is [*sic*] transformed from being a personal problem into being everyone's problem, or at least anyone within organizational reach. There is a combined power to be found in refusing the circumstances of a loss while then also expressing that refusal in a way that demands its visibility when both the refusal and the public expression of grief are regarded as things that should not be happening." (2021, 29)

This gestures toward the significance of processing catastrophe-related trauma in a collective context. Even catastrophes that seem random affect more than the individual victim. They impact those closest to them and the communities of which they are a part—their neighborhoods, their friendship networks, and their social bonds. To empower those who are grieving, feminists frequently "reimagine mourning," transforming it from "a process of individualized grief-work" to "a collective condition" (Brown and Puri 2022, 308).

————

In this volume, we take a feminist approach to public catastrophes and their effects. We build on the work of the Institute for Research on Women during the 2018–2019 academic year, when "Public Catastrophes, Private Losses" was our annual theme. Four of the five chapters featured in this volume originated from events held as part of IRW's Distinguished Lecture Series that year. Naomi Klein gave the keynote lecture in our "Public Catastrophes" series. A version of her talk on the climate catastrophe appears as chapter 1 in this volume. Chapter 2 is an edited transcript of a conversation about slavery and its afterlives that features Marisa J. Fuentes, Christina Sharpe, and Michelle Commander. Activist Jennifer Flynn Walker spoke at an IRW panel on drugs, criminalization, and social justice; in chapter 3 she writes with legal scholar Bela August Walker about the pernicious effects of the opioid epidemic. The late activist Carmen Vázquez spoke at an IRW panel on the aftermath of AIDS; in chapter 4, with historian Marcia M. Gallo, she compares the devastating onset of AIDS with the first few months of COVID-19. The final chapter, curated by Kathleen C. Riley, is a series of interwoven vignettes by former IRW Seminar Fellows Smruthi Bala Kannan, Stacy S. Klein, Ellen Malenas Ledoux, Basuli Deb, L. Amede Obiora—and Riley herself. It discusses the privations and private losses incurred during the COVID-19 lockdown.

"Climate change is a risk multiplier," writes activist Naomi Klein in "Labor of Loss: Climate Change and the Emerging Economy of Care and Repair," emphasizing the heightened risk that already vulnerable communities confront due to the climate crisis. Klein rejects neoliberal policies that privatize loss and blame people for their own suffering. Instead, she calls for broad, responsive policy solutions like the Green New Deal, which refuse to pit the economic against the social and demonstrate that "we are in this together." Klein is inspired by the way that young environmental movement leaders like Greta Thunberg give public expression to their sense of sadness, loss, and anger in the face of climate degradation. She hopes that a reinvigorated environmental movement that begins from "an admission of loss" will help transform our "extractive" mentality into one that is motivated by "an ethos of care and repair"—both for the natural world and its inhabitants.

Traumatic experiences of slavery travel through time and space, affecting the study of the past as well as the present. "Slavery's Shadows: The Afterlife of Dispossession" captures this dynamic in a conversation between scholars Marisa J. Fuentes and Christina Sharpe, with commentary by Michelle Commander. Fuentes discusses her book *Dispossessed Lives*, a history of enslaved Black women in Barbados, as well as a new project on "refuse" slaves, those who were rejected at purchase or who died before they could be sold. She argues that both projects call for "an ethical method to tell silent stories" which avoids the gratuitous replication of violence and seeks instead to "do no harm." Similarly, Christina Sharpe tries not to leave Black people "in a register of abandonment." In her book *In the Wake*, Sharpe "weave[s] together images, current catastrophes, and quotidian events and literature to understand the ways that slavery's still unresolved unfoldings are constitutive of the contemporary conditions of Black being." Her work demonstrates that while Black people may be "constituted through vulnerability," they imagine and construct other ways of being in the world, in the day-to-day, through strategies of care and refusal.

The legacy of slavery persists in the systems that perpetuate structural racism in the United States. In "The Cruelty Is the Point: Women and Children as Weapons in the War on Drugs," Jennifer Flynn Walker and Bela August Walker describe how the opioid epidemic compounds pre-existing catastrophes. Their focus is the child welfare system, which was transformed by the Adoption and Safe Families Act of 1997. This legislation created a bureaucratic apparatus that disproportionately surveils and punishes African Americans—a propensity that has only increased since the opioid epidemic began. "By the time they are eighteen," Flynn Walker and August Walker write, "over fifty percent of Black children will have been subject to a child welfare investigation." Many of these children have been separated from their parents and placed in foster care, practices inflicting untold trauma on African American families. Advocating for the abolition of Child Protective Services (CPS), the authors call upon us to respond to the opioid epidemic with harm reduction programs as well as housing and employment services. "Substance use disorder is a public health crisis," they write. "Families that are impacted should be treated the same way as a family impacted by cancer: with love, support, and money"—not with punishment.

Love and loss are two pervasive themes of Marcia M. Gallo and Carmen Vázquez's chapter, "Memories of Two Pandemics." This chapter juxtaposes the emergence of HIV/AIDS in San Francisco with the early days of the COVID-19 pandemic through a series of entwined journal entries. The authors demonstrate the "malfeasance" of both former President Reagan's response to HIV/AIDS and ex-President Trump's refusal to acknowledge the dangers of COVID-19. Gallo and Vázquez also document how the "two devastatingly cruel crises" of HIV/AIDS and COVID-19 have inflicted crushing personal losses on Americans who are gay, "old, poor or people of color." Their particular focus is a group San Francisco–based LGBTQ activists who in the 1980s "were part of vibrant and resilient . . . and progressive communities with local, national, and international influence." Many of these people were close friends or family to the authors. Part social history, part memoir, this chapter is a heartfelt lamentation for lives prematurely lost.

In the final chapter in this volume, "Skin and Screen: A Collaborative Take on Touch in the Time of COVID," a group of scholars who experienced the COVID-19 lockdown in countries as varied as India, Italy, Nigeria, and the United States ponder the relationship between "the skin, a permeable boundary between self and other, and the screen, a two-dimensional conduit for continued sociality and 'staying in touch.'" The scholars—Kathleen C. Riley, Smruthi Bala Kannan, Stacy S. Klein, Ellen Malenas Ledoux, Basuli Deb, and L. Amede Obiora—write a series of interwoven vignettes that address skin and screen in relation to etymology (in English and Igbo), pandemic parenting, sex and intimacy during COVID-19, and teaching over Zoom. Mostly (but not entirely) lamenting life transformed by the lack of sensory touch, they explore how the use of technology during lockdown has reshaped the contours of our domestic and professional worlds. The authors observe that COVID-19 has exposed "the interdependence of humanity's oneness or figurative 'skin'" (Obiora) but also express a "growing foreboding" about our capacity to transcend parochial priorities in pandemic times.

————

When the United States reached 500,000 COVID deaths in February 2021, President Joe Biden gave a heartfelt speech in which he told the public: "The people we lost were extraordinary. They spanned generations. . . . Just like that, so many of them took [their] final breath alone, in America. . . . We ask you to join us to remember, so we can heal; to find purpose in the work ahead; to show that there is light in the darkness." He warned of the costs of complacency in the face of such staggering loss. "While we have been fighting this pandemic for so long, we have to resist becoming numb to the sorrow. . . . We have to resist viewing each life as a . . . statistic or a blur or on the news" (Biden 2021).

President Biden and his wife, and Vice President Harris and her husband, stood in front of 500 candles honoring the dead, using their own bodies to symbolize the body politic. They urged Americans to come together in grief, acknowledging the public nature of losses that are often seen as private. They recognized that disruptive events, COVID among them, destroy individual lives and have a ripple effect on those around them.

The experience of COVID compels us to reflect on the ongoing AIDS epidemic, which has already killed approximately 700,000 Americans and far more people globally. The Centers for Disease Control and Prevention (CDC) reports that from 2017 to 2021, more than 30,000 people in the United States were diagnosed with HIV each year, the majority of whom were gay men of color living in the South, a region where HIV care is notoriously poor (CDC 2012; see also Masiano et al. 2019). Although AIDS continues to take the lives of thousands of people in the United States each year, the epidemic has never received adequate national attention as a public health emergency. Nor is it adequately memorialized. As Aldarondo et al. eloquently put it, "the space occupied by the AIDS crisis in our national memory is disproportionately tiny relative to its horrors" (2020, 189). The National AIDS Memorial Grove in San Francisco's Golden Gate Park is the only federally designated AIDS memorial in the country. Congress passed legislation to provide the memorial with this status in 1996, but to this day it receives no government funding; volunteers created and continue to sustain the site.

The example of AIDS—and the chapters in this volume—indicate that memory is not simply something that belongs to individuals; it is created in group contexts and shaped by politics and power. Groups that hold power have the capacity to define what we know about the past. Yet, at certain moments, dominant understandings of the past are contested. When survivors of public catastrophes tell stories about their lives and the communities of which they are a part, they also create opportunities to forge new solidarities.

Experiencing catastrophe may also precipitate new ways of existing in and engaging with the world. Alexis Pauline Gumbs writes that people who survived the transatlantic slave trade learned something important about how to breathe in the unbearable conditions of the ship's hold. Today Black Americans continue "breathing in unbreathable circumstances . . . in the chokehold of racial gendered ableist capitalism" (2021, 21). We should study marine life, Gumbs argues, especially those creatures who, like us, are mammals. These creatures have "much to teach us about the vulnerability, collaboration, and adaptation we need in order to be with the change at this time" (22). Crucially, marine mammals have learned how to breathe differently underwater in order not to drown. What if, as Gumbs asks, in this era of chokeholds, climate catastrophe, and a breath-denying virus, we teach ourselves "another way to breathe?" (21).

Notes

1. Deaths from the virus were most frequently located in areas associated with "poverty, racism, and overpolicing." "People were getting sick from this new virus because of where they lived," Steven Thrasher notes in his book *The Viral Underclass*, "they were dying disproportionately from it because of the bodies they had been living in their whole lives" (2022, 5).

2. ACT-UP was the most visible—although not the only—activist group to loudly politicize queer grief, and often used "postmodern, confrontational" tactics (Juhasz 2012, 72). It has been criticized for being an activist organization primarily populated by white, middle-class gay men and for giving short shrift to women, trans folk, and people of color whose activism took a range of different forms (Alvarez, cited in Aldarondo et al.

2020). The lives of queer people of color at the AIDS epidemic's center have often been seen as less worthy than those of their white, straight, male, cisgender counterparts.

References

Ahmed, Sara. 2004. *The Cultural Politics of Emotion*. Edinburgh: University of Edinburgh Press.

Aldarondo, Celia, Roger Hallas, Pablo Alvarez, Jim Hubbard, Dredge Byung'chu Kang-Nguyễn, and Jih-Fei Cheng. 2020. "Dispatches from the Pasts/Memories of AIDS." In *AIDS and the Distribution of Crises*, edited by Jih-Fei Cheng, Alexandra Juhasz, and Nishant Shahani, 183–216. Durham, NC: Duke University Press.

Almasy, Steve, and Laura Ly. 2017. "Flint Water Crisis: Report Says 'Systemic Racism' Played Role." *CNN*, February 18, 2017. https://www.cnn.com/2017/02/18/politics/flint-water-report -systemic-racism/index.html.

Athanasiou, Athena. 2006. "Reflections on the Politics of Mourn- ing: Feminist Ethics and Politics in the Age of Empire." *Historein* 5: 40–57. https://doi.org/10.12681/historein.72.

Berry, Maya J. 2021. "In Mourning: Sociocultural Anthropology in 2020." *American Anthropologist* 123, no. 4 (December): 931–947. https://doi.org/10.1111/aman.13662.

Biden, Joseph R. 2021. "Remarks by President Biden on the More Than 500,000 American Lives Lost to COVID-19." White House, February 22, 2021. https://www.whitehouse.gov /briefing-room/speeches-remarks/2021/02/22/remarks-by -president-biden-on-the-more-than-500000-american-lives -lost-to-covid-19/.

Bonilla, Yarimar. 2020. "The Coloniality of Disaster: Race, Empire, and the Temporal Logics of Emergency in Puerto Rico, USA." *Political Geography* 78 (April): 10218. https://doi.org/10.1016/j .polgeo.2020.102181.

Brown, Kimberly Juanita, and Jyoti Puri. 2022. "The Uses of
    Mourning: An Introduction." *Meridians: Feminism, Race,
    Transnationalism* 21, no. 2 (October): 307–316.

Butler, Judith. 2004. *Precarious Life: The Powers of Mourning and
    Violence*. New York: Verso.

CalFire. 2020. "2020 Incident Archive." https://www.fire.ca.gov
    /incidents/2020.

———. 2021. "2021 Incident Archive." https://www.fire.ca.gov
    /incidents/2021.

Campbell, Maeve. 2021. "'The Global South is Not on the Front
    Page but It Is on the Front Line': Meet Vanessa Nakate."
    Euronews. https://www.euronews.com/green/2021/11/05/vanessa
    -nakate-the-global-south-is-not-on-the-front-page-but-it-is-on
    -the-front-line.

Caruth, Cathy, ed. 1995. *Trauma: Explorations in Memory*. Baltimore,
    MD: Johns Hopkins University Press.

Catlin, Jonathon. 2022. "Slow Catastrophe: A Concept for the
    Anthropocene." In *The Environmental Apocalypse: Interdisciplin-
    ary Reflections on the Climate Crisis*, edited by Jakub Kowalewski,
    51–68. London: Routledge.

Celermajer, Danielle. 2021. *Summertime: Reflections on a Vanishing
    Future*. Sydney: Penguin Random House.

Center for Disaster Philanthropy. 2020. "2019–2020 Australian
    Bushfires." https://disasterphilanthropy.org/disasters/2019
    -australian-wildfires/.

Centers for Disease Control and Prevention (CDC). 2021. "HIV
    Surveillance Report." https://www.cdc.gov/hiv-data/nhss
    /estimated-hiv-incidence-and-prevalence.html?CDC_AAref_Val.

Christian, Jenna Marie, and Lorraine Dowler. 2019. "Slow and Fast
    Violence: A Feminist Critique of Binaries." *ACME: An
    International Journal for Critical Geographies* 18 (5): 1066–1075.

Craps, Stef. 2020. "Climate Trauma." In *The Routledge Companion to
    Literature and Trauma*, edited by Colin Davis and Hanna
    Meretoja, 275–284. Abingdon, UK: Routledge.

———. 2023. "Ecological Mourning: Living With Loss in the Anthropocene." In *Critical Memory Studies: New Approaches*, edited by Brett Ashley Kaplan, 69–77. New York: Bloomsbury.

Danylevich, Theodora, and Alyson Patsavas. 2021. "Introduction: Cripistemologies of Crisis: Emergent Knowledges for the Present." *Lateral: Journal of the Cultural Studies Association* 10, no. 1 (Spring): https://csalateral.org/section/cripistemologies-of -crisis/introduction-emergent-knowledges-for-the-present -danylevich-patsavas/.

Erikson, Kai. 1995. "Notes on Trauma and Community." In *Trauma: Explorations in Memory*, edited by Cathy Caruth, 183–199. Baltimore, MD: Johns Hopkins University Press.

Farr, Brittany. 2022. "Grief and Black Feminist Theory." *Balkinization* (blog), February 2, 2022. https://balkin.blogspot.com/2022 /02/grief-and-black-feminist-theory.html.

Fedinick, Kristi Pullen, Steve Taylor, and Michele Roberts. 2019. *Watered Down Justice*. New York: National Resources Defense Council. https://www.nrdc.org/sites/default/files/watered-down -justice-report.pdf.

Fleetwood, Nicole R., and Rachel Kushner. 2020. "Carceral Aesthetics." *Artforum* 59, no. 1 (September). https://www.artforum.com /print/202007/nicole-r-fleetwood-in-conversation-with-rachel -kushner-83681.

France 24. 2023. "In Pictures: Canada Wildfires Shroud New York in Apocalyptic Smog." June 8, 2023. https://www.france24.com /en/americas/20230608-in-pictures-canada-wildfires-shroud -new-york-in-apocalyptic-smog.

Gessen, Masha. 2020. "Judith Butler Wants Us to Reshape Our Rage." *New Yorker,* February 9, 2020. https://www.newyorker .com/culture/the-new-yorker-interview/judith-butler-wants-us -to-reshape-our-rage.

Grandi, Filippo. 2021. "Climate Change is an Emergency for Everyone, Everywhere." UNCHR. November 9, 2021. https:// www.unhcr.org/news/.

Gumbs, Alexis Pauline. 2021. "Undrowned: Black Feminist Lessons from Marine Mammals." *Soundings: A Journal of Politics and Culture* 78 (Summer): 20–37. https://www.doi.org/10.3898/SOUN.78.01.2021.

Hartman, Saidiya. 2002. "The Time of Slavery." *South Atlantic Quarterly* 101, no. 4 (Fall): 757–777.

Hickel, Jason. 2020. "Quantifying National Responsibility for Climate Breakdown: An Equality-Based Attribution Approach for Carbon Dioxide Emissions in Excess of the Planetary Boundary." *The Lancet* 4, no. 9 (September): e399–e404. https://doi.org/10.1016/S2542-5196(20)30196-0.

Hill, Barry E. 2021. "Human Rights, Environmental Justice, and Climate Change: Flint, Michigan." American Bar Association, June 14, 2021. https://www.americanbar.org/groups/crsj/publications/human_rights_magazine_home/the-truth-about-science/human-rights-environmental-justice-and-climate-change/.

Juhasz, Alexandra. 2012. "Forgetting ACT UP." *Quarterly Journal of Speech* 98, no. 1 (February): 69–74.

Lifton, Robert. 1971. *History and Human Survival: Essays on the Young and Old, Survivors and the Dead, Peace and War, and on Contemporary Psychohistory.* New York: Vintage.

Longo, Sophia Rose. 2021. "Even as a Dream: Feminist and Queer Grief, Ritual, and Futurity." MA thesis, San Francisco State University. https://scholarworks.calstate.edu/downloads/f7623j62n.

Masiano, Steven P., Erika G. Martin, Rose S. Bono, Bassam Dahman, Lindsay M. Sabik, Faye Z. Belgrave, Adaora A. Adimora, and April D. Kimmel. 2019. "Suboptimal Geographic Accessibility to Comprehensive HIV Care in the US: Regional and Urban-Rural Differences." *Journal of the International AIDS Society* 22, no. 5 (May): e25286. https://doi.10.1002/jia2.25286.

McKibben, Bill. 1989. *The End of Nature.* New York: Random House.

Mortimer-Sandilands, Catriona. 2010. "Melancholy Natures, Queer Ecologies." In *Queer Ecologies: Sex, Nature, Politics, Desire*, edited by Catriona Mortimer-Sandilands and Bruce Erickson, 331–358. Bloomington: Indiana University Press.

Movement for Black Lives (M4BL). 2020. "The Preamble." https://m4bl.org/policy-platforms/the-preamble/.

Nellis, Ashley. 2021. "The Color of Justice: Racial and Ethnic Disparity in State Prisons." The Sentencing Project, October 13, 2021. https://www.sentencingproject.org/reports/the-color-of -justice-racial-and-ethnic-disparity-in-state-prisons-the -sentencing-project/.

Nixon, Rob. 2011. *Slow Violence and the Environmentalism of the Poor*. Cambridge, MA: Harvard University Press.

O'Sullivan, Feargus. 2022. "The World's Fastest-Growing Cities Are Facing the Most Climate Risk." *Bloomberg*, February 28, 2022. https://www.bloomberg.com/news/articles/2022-02-28 /global-south-cities-face-dire-climate-impacts-un-report.

Oxford English Dictionary (OED). n.d. "Catastrophe, Noun." https://www.oed.com/dictionary/catastrophe_n?tab=meaning _and_use#10077081.

Perkins, Ben. 2022. "Slow Violence and the Politics of Representation of Ecocide." *Environmental Humanities* 14, no. 3 (November): 564–570. https://doi.org/10.1215/22011919-9962860.

Rankine, Claudia. 2015. "The Condition of Black Life Is One of Mourning." *New York Times*, June 22, 2015. https://www.nytimes .com/2015/06/22/magazine/the-condition-of-black-life-is-one-of -mourning.html.

Readfearn, Graham, and Adam Morton. 2020. "Almost 3 Billion Animals Affected by Australian Bushfires, Report Shows." *The Guardian*, July 28, 2020. https://www.theguardian.com /environment/2020/jul/28/almost-3-billion-animals-affected-by -australian-megafires-report-shows-aoe.

Remes, Jacob A. C., and Andy Horowitz. 2021. *Critical Disaster Studies*. Philadelphia: University of Pennsylvania Press.

Richardson, Allisa V. 2017. "Bearing Witness while Black: Theoriz-
    ing African American Mobile Journalism after Ferguson."
    Digital Journalism 5 (6): 673–698. https://doi.org/10.1080/21670811
    .2016.1193818.

Sawyer, Wendy, and Peter Wagner. 2023. "Mass Incarceration: The
    Whole Pie 2023." Prison Policy Initiative, March 14, 2023.
    https://www.prisonpolicy.org/reports/pie2023.html.

Sharpe, Christina. 2016. *In the Wake: On Blackness and Being.*
    Durham, NC: Duke University Press.

Sierra Praeli, Yvette. 2022. "'Only the Rains Will Stop It': Bolivia
    Forest Fires Hit Protected Areas." Translated by Sydney Sims.
    Mongabay, January 7, 2022. https://news.mongabay.com/2022/01
    /only-the-rains-will-stop-it-bolivia-forest-fires-hit-protected
    -areas/.

Smith, Jamil. 2015. "Black Lives Matter Co-Founder: 'We Are in a
    State of Emergency.'" *New Republic*, July 20, 2015. https://
    newrepublic.com/article/122334/blacklivesmatter-co-founder-we
    -are-state-emergency.

Stein, Arlene. 2014. *Reluctant Witnesses: Survivors, Their Children,
    and the Rise of Holocaust Consciousness.* Oxford: Oxford Univer-
    sity Press.

Sultana, Farhana. 2021. "Critical Climate Justice." *Geographical
    Journal* 188, no. 1 (March): 118–124. https://doi.org/10.1111/geoj
    .12417.

———. 2022. "The Unbearable Heaviness of Climate Coloniality."
    Political Geography 99 (November): 102638. https://doi.org/10
    .1016/j.polgeo.2022.102638.

Thrasher, Steven W. 2022. *The Viral Underclass: The Human Toll when
    Inequality and Disease Collide.* New York: Macmillan.

Tuana, Nancy. 2019. "Climate Apartheid: The Forgetting of Race in
    the Anthropocene." *Critical Philosophy of Race* 7 (1): 1–31.

United Nations Environment Program. n.d. "Responding to
    Climate Change." https://www.unep.org/regions/africa/regional
    -initiatives/responding-climate-change.

Verlie, Blanche. 2022. *Learning to Live With Climate Change: From Anxiety to Transformation*. New York: Routledge.

Wang, Leah. 2023. "Punishment beyond Prisons 2023: Incarceration and Supervision by State." Prison Policy Initiative, May 2023. https://www.prisonpolicy.org/reports/correctionalcontrol2023.html.

Wintour, Patrick. 2021. "'Apocalyse Soon': Reluctant Middle East Forced to Open Eyes to Climate Crisis." *The Guardian*, October 29, 2021. https://www.theguardian.com/environment/2021/oct/29/apocalypse-soon-reluctant-middle-east-forced-to-open-eyes-to-climate-crisis.

1

Labor of Loss

Climate Change and the Emerging Economy of Care and Repair

NAOMI KLEIN

In the twenty-first century, there is no shortage of climate-change-related catastrophes. Massive flooding has displaced hundreds of thousands of people in Mozambique, Zimbabwe, and southern India. In the United States we can point to Hurricanes Katrina, Harvey, Michael, Maria and Irma; record-breaking wildfires in California; and flooding in the Midwest. These are only a few examples. For the most part, media coverage focuses on the most visible losses related to these events—the profound stresses of displacement, as well as the economic costs of destroyed homes, damaged infrastructure, and disaster response and relief. The human cost of all this is usually discussed in highly disembodied terms. We focus on the hard data: the number of people dead in the aftermath of disasters or the number of people forced to move as a result of drought or erosion.[1]

We explore the intimate and psychological losses linked to climate change all too rarely. Yet we know that the total loss of control in the face of fearsome weather events is a tremendously traumatic experience. So is the frantic loss of communication with loved ones and not knowing if they are alive or dead—something millions of Puerto Ricans experienced on the island and in the diaspora when communication networks went down during and after Hurricane Maria. There can also be a lost sense of dignity when privacy is stripped away by television cameras in search of dramatic visuals. Many also describe a loss of pride when days are spent pleading with the cold and complex bureaucracies of insurance companies, creditors, the Federal Emergency Management Agency (FEMA), and other organizations.

Media coverage of disasters also rarely focuses on the loss of safety that comes when domestic abuse intensifies in the aftermath of disasters, as it often does (O'Neil 2016; Parkinson 2019; Vigaud-Walsh 2019; WHO 2005). Indeed, all of these costs and losses are born unevenly: the already wealthy have gold-plated insurance policies and stand to increase their wealth in the aftermath of disasters (Hersher 2019). The less wealthy and poorly insured—particularly in the Black and Latinx communities—are far more likely to lose whatever wealth they managed to accumulate before these disasters. In less developed countries many low-income people do not have official title to the lands they have lived on for generations, so when it comes time to rebuild, they frequently lose their land altogether. This is true in parts of the United States as well, particularly Puerto Rico (Acevedo and Pacheco 2018). These are some of the ways that climate change exacerbates and deepens pre-existing inequalities, but there are many more.

All of this contributed to the epidemic of despair following Hurricane Maria in Puerto Rico, reflected in the huge spike in calls to the island's 24-hour mental health hotline. The storm hit in September 2017. According to a government report, more than 3,000 people who called the hotline between November 2017 and January 2018 reported having already attempted suicide—a 246 percent increase over the previous year (Campbell 2018). These are some of the private losses that flow from public catastrophes.

There are collective ones as well—profound psychological and cultural losses that set in when one's homeland is altered to such a degree that home becomes unrecognizable. A decade and a half ago, Australian philosopher and professor of sustainability Glenn Albrecht coined a term to capture the particular form of psychological distress that sets in when the lands that we love, and from which we take comfort and form identity, are changed so much that they become alienating and unfamiliar. He defines "solastalgia" as "the homesickness you have when you are still at home" (Albrecht 2012). The condition is often "exacerbated by a sense of powerlessness or lack of control over the unfolding change process" (Albrecht et al. 2007).

This is particularly acute for Indigenous people, whose cultures are intensely land-based. For my 2014 book *This Changes Everything*, I interviewed the Anishinaabe scholar and artist Leanne Simpson. She talked about how collecting the sap from maple trees is a millennia-old practice in her people's way of life in what is now Southern Ontario. But climate-change-related shifts in weather patterns mean that, in some years, the sap doesn't flow, or flows at the wrong time. These facts alter her people's relationship to the land and the exercise of land rights in fundamental ways—an immeasurable loss that is, once again, more private than public.

Albrecht argues that in the era of climate disruption, with daily news of seasons turned upside down, insect apocalypses, glacier melt and coral death, solastalgia is fast becoming a universal psychological state—and it is no longer just linked to particular geographies. He writes that "a feeling of global dread asserts itself as the planet heats and our climate gets more hostile and unpredictable" (Albrecht 2012). This distress is still felt most by those immediately impacted by climate disruption: those living in low-lying coastal areas or island nations, or whose homes rest on melting permafrost. But it lurks in the background for all of us.

Meanwhile, many young people in the climate movement describe a different, though related, feeling—a great homesickness for a future they thought they would have, but which is disappearing with every day that adults fail to treat climate change as an emergency. So far, we lack the research to fully understand how this is impacting youth mental health. But anecdotal evidence abounds. To cite just one example, a few weeks ago, I gave a talk, and the first question was from a young woman soliciting my opinion on whether or not she should have kids. Did I think she should, or was the world likely to be so dangerous that it really wasn't a fair choice to make? I told her that no one can answer that for her. Yet I get asked this question with increasing frequency at similar events, sometimes quietly, during book signings. There should be no shame in wanting to voice these uncertainties—these are the kinds of questions that the hard scientific facts of climate change quite logically raise. Should I have kids? What will happen to my kids? Where should I live? If my community is evacuated suddenly, how will I help my aging parent? How will my own or my partner's disability impact my chances of getting to safety? How will I get my medications? My hormone treatments? How do I tell my young child about climate change without giving them nightmares?

These are intimate questions that we should be grappling with together as a society that is facing a massive collective crisis. Yet so many of the fears, losses, and traumas of public catastrophes are borne privately, even shamefully. We catch glimpses of what these personal quandaries look like some-times. For instance, a photograph of nursing home residents near Houston, who were waist-deep in water, went viral after Hurricane Harvey caused mass flooding in the state (Fortin 2017). This vulnerability fits a pattern. During Superstorm Sandy, elderly and disabled people who lived on the higher floors of public housing projects in the Rockaways and Sunset Park were stranded for weeks without electricity or water. These residents were overwhelmingly Black and Latinx (Rugh 2013), exposing the intersectional nature of climate vulnerabilities.

Here is the hard truth: the people who are being left behind in our society every day—with no catastrophic event required—face exponentially increased risks when climate-related shocks arrive. Climate change is a risk multiplier. We need collective responses and solutions to these facts. We need policy that addresses the core question this raises: How are we going to care for one another during extreme and shock-laden times? What values are going to govern our societies as we enter the era of climate disruption? Will it be *survival of the fittest*? Or will it be *no one is disposable*? If we ignore the reality of climate change's many private losses, the former will prevail by default.

Meanwhile, we continue to privatize the burdens of these public catastrophes, blaming victims and seeking individual solutions. "You should have bought flood insurance," we hear. Or "You need an evacuation plan for your family." Or, if you are forced to migrate, "You should have gone through the proper channels." This is what neoliberal capitalism does—it turns the collective crises it produces into individual burdens.

Meanwhile, we barely have a language to discuss the profound emotions raised by our historical moment—by the knowledge of what we have already lost of the natural world that sustains us, and of how little time remains to change course. For much of the environmental movement, the theory of change has been pretty simple: scare people with the facts and try to harness that fear to turn them into activists. To put it more specifically: put out a picture of a polar bear on a melting ice flow, then ask people to sign a petition (and then make a donation). This is done with the best of intentions, and to fund important work. But, as a movement, we have done a poor job of creating space for people to express and work through the complex range of emotions evoked by our ecological crisis, including climate grief and sorrow.

Thankfully, this is starting to change. We are starting to see another model for how to build a movement, one that leads with an admission of loss. The person most publicly embodying this very different approach is Greta Thunberg, the Swedish teenager who has kick-started a global youth movement demanding transformative climate action. Thunberg speaks very openly about her own personal story: how, at age eleven, she was so grief-stricken by the climate crisis that she stopped eating and talking (Thunberg 2018). With her activism she has helped thousands of other young people to find their own ways of speaking from a place of honest grief and righteous fury, producing public expressions of what were previously private losses.

There is also something else happening that cannot be underestimated: for the first time, there are political responses to the climate crisis being discussed that are on a similar scale to the crisis. Responses that are not technocratic, but ones that are bold and transformational. Responses like the Green New Deal. The Green New Deal resolution put forward by Congresswoman Alexandria Ocasio-Cortez calls for transforming the economy to get off fossil fuels in a decade, parallel to the key time frame of the original New Deal in the 1930s. It is anchored in a huge job-creation plan. The Green

New Deal also importantly takes a rights-based approach: a right to clean air, clean water, and healthy food. This approach is particularly resonant in places like Flint, Michigan, or Trenton, New Jersey, because we know that the health impacts of industry are overwhelmingly experienced by Black and Brown communities. Crucially, the Green New Deal also emphasizes frontline leadership: the people who got the worst deal under our current extractive economy must help write the policy, and benefit from the jobs and robust green services it creates. The convergence of these forces—the global youth climate movement and these large-scale policy proposals—is proving a potent and energizing combination. Climate action is no longer just about averting catastrophe in the future, it is also now understood as a key to unlocking a better present—one that is fairer, more humane, more caring. Which means that there is still peril, but there is now also promise.

The most common critique of the Green New Deal is that it is trying to do too much, or that it is a laundry list of everything the political left has ever wanted, painted green. In making the Green New Deal about social and economic transformation, critics argue that it is exponentially harder to enact than, say, a simple carbon tax or cap-and-trade scheme that moderate Republicans might back. These assertions, however, reflect a failure to grapple with those private, unequally distributed, intersectional losses that I outlined earlier.

Let us look at the claim that a limited focus on a carbon tax or carbon trading would be more likely to sail through Congress. There have been attempts to introduce market-based climate policies delinked from racial or economic justice since the Clinton administration, and they have all been defeated. In 1997, Vice President Al Gore and President Bill Clinton lobbied hard for carbon trading, rather than firm regulations and caps, to be written into the Kyoto Protocol

(Royden 2002). Europe reluctantly agreed, because it seemed as if that was what it would take to get the world's largest economy to sign on. And then the U.S. Congress refused to ratify the agreement, leaving the rest of the world hanging. During the Obama administration, an attempt to introduce a federal cap-and-trade plan failed as well, in large part because of Obama's decision to prioritize health care instead (Lehmann and Chemnick 2017).

One lesson we can take from this history is that a narrow approach is not necessarily more pragmatic. Politicians do not pay a political price for failing to enact climate policies that focus solely on carbon pricing because the public either does not understand them or is convinced that these policies will do nothing but raise the cost of their gas and electricity bills. This last concern is not one that should be lightly dismissed. We live in a time of extraordinary wealth inequality where working people have already lost a huge amount of security on the altar of neoliberal austerity. Jobs are precarious. Public services have been cut to the bone. Which may help explain why, around the world, working people are showing that they are unwilling to bear the burden of climate action while the elites who profited so handsomely from creating the crisis are not sharing that burden.

On the other hand, linking climate action to policies that tangibly improve lives and reduce financial stresses—like universal health care and a jobs guarantee—makes climate action more politically sellable, not less. It is understandable that people are more immediately concerned with making ends meet and whether or not they have health care than saving the world. What the Green New Deal says is: you don't have to choose. Our overlapping social and ecological crises do not need to be pitted against each other. They can all be addressed under a holistic vision for a post-extractive economy.

This brings us to the "laundry list" critique. For some reason it is difficult for many of our most prominent pundits to understand what having a good healthcare system has to do with climate change, or what having your labor rights protected has to do with climate action (both are included in the Green New Deal resolution). But none of this is complicated. If we think about Puerto Rico once again, more than 3,000 people died after Hurricane Maria, but the major cause of death was not falling debris—it was a healthcare system and an electricity system that had been cut to the bone before Maria, and which were totally unable to cope with the stress of a Category 5 storm (Dreisbach 2019). A lot of the five-star resorts weathered the storm just fine. The schools and hospitals did not. We learn this lesson again and again after disasters: it is not the weather itself that is most lethal, but the intersection of heavy weather and a weak and neglected public sphere. There is little that would save more lives in future climate-change-intensified disasters than a functioning, fully funded universal healthcare system.

Let's turn to the labor involved in helping people heal and cope with trauma after these events. The workers on the front lines are nurses, home health aides, and mental health workers who staff suicide prevention hotlines. This care work is overwhelmingly work done by women (Oxfam International 2020). Teachers and artists also do critical psychological work in the aftermath of disasters, bringing a sense of normalcy to young people's lives and helping students to process their emotions and cope with loss collectively. All of this care work is part of coping with climate change and minimizing the less visible losses. It is the labor that takes those private risks and treats them as collective, that spreads the burdens out more equally and tells people that we are in this together. Something that is very rarely mentioned is that these care jobs are also green jobs. Teaching does not burn a lot of carbon. Childcare does not burn a lot of carbon. Nursing does not burn a lot of carbon. Making art does not burn a lot of carbon. In a warming world, we need to invest in these sectors as never before and reimagine them so they are even less polluting.

Fundamentally, climate action is about how we are going to treat one another, and we urgently need to find truly intersectional solutions. Ocasio-Cortez's congressional resolution hints at this potential.[2] It calls for creating well-paying jobs, "restoring and protecting threatened, endangered, and fragile ecosystems," as well as "cleaning up existing hazardous waste and abandoned sites, ensuring economic development and sustainability on those sites." There are many such sites across the United States, entire landscapes that have been left to waste after they were no longer useful to frackers, miners, and drillers. They are sacrifice zones. This "organized abandonment" is a lot like how our culture treats people: as eminently sacrifice-able. It is what has been done to so many workers in the neoliberal period, who are used up and then abandoned to addiction and despair. As Ruth Wilson Gilmore (2007) and Mariame Kaba (2013) have told us, this is the logic at the center of the carceral state: huge sectors of the population are more economically useful as prison laborers, or numbers on the spreadsheet of a private prison, than they are as free workers.

There is a grand holistic story to be told here about the duty to repair—to repair our relationship with the earth and with one another, to heal the deep wounds dating back to the founding of the country. While it is true that climate change is a crisis produced by an excess of greenhouse gases in the atmosphere, it is also in a more profound sense a crisis produced by an extractive mindset—a way of viewing both the natural world and the majority of its inhabitants as resources to use up and then discard. It is what I call the "gig and dig" economy. I firmly believe that we will not emerge from this crisis without a shift in worldview, a transformation from "gig and dig" to an ethos of care and repair.

Notes

1. This chapter is adapted from a speech given as a part of the Institute for Research on Women's 2018–2019 Distinguished Lecture Series "Public Catastrophes, Private Losses." The speech took place in New Brunswick, New Jersey, on April 4, 2019.
2. See H.R. 109, 116th Cong. (2019) and H. Res. 332, 117th Cong. (2021).

References

Acevedo, Nicole, and Istra Pacheco. 2018. "No Deeds, No Aid to Rebuild Homes: Puerto Rico's Reconstruction Challenge." *NBC News*, May 8, 2018. https://www.nbcnews.com/storyline/puerto -rico-crisis/no-deeds-no-aid-rebuild-homes-puerto-rico-s -reconstruction-n868396.

Albrecht, Glenn. 2012. "The Age of Solastalgia." *The Conversation*, August 7, 2012. http://theconversation.com/the-age-of -solastalgia-8337.

Albrecht, Glenn, Gina-Maree Sartore, Linda Connor, Nick Higginbotham, Sonia Freeman, Brian Kelly, Helen Stain, Anne Tonna, and Georgia Pollard. 2007. "Solastalgia: The Distress Caused by Environmental Change." *Australasian Psychiatry* 15 (suppl. 1): S95–98. https://doi.org/10.1080 /10398560701701288.

Campbell, Alexia Fernández. 2018. "Calls to Puerto Rico's Suicide Hotline Have Skyrocketed since Hurricane Maria." *Vox*, February 21, 2018. https://www.vox.com/policy-and-politics/2018 /2/21/17032168/puerto-rico-suicide-hotline-hurricane-maria.

Dreisbach, Tom. 2019. "Problems with Health Care Contributed to Hurricane Maria Death Toll in Puerto Rico." *All Things Considered*, NPR, February 21, 2019. https://www.npr.org/2019/02/21/696769824/problems-with-health-care-contributed-to-hurricane-maria-death-toll-in-puerto-ri.

Fortin, Jacey. 2017. "Behind the Photo of the Older Women in Waist-High Water in Texas." *New York Times*, August 28, 2017. https://www.nytimes.com/2017/08/28/us/nursing-home-houston-texas.html.

Gilmore, Ruth Wilson. 2007. *Golden Gulag: Prisons, Surplus, Crisis, and Opposition in Globalizing California*. Oakland: University of California Press.

Hersher, Rebeca. 2019. "How Federal Disaster Money Favors the Rich." *NPR*, March 5, 2019. https://www.npr.org/2019/03/05/688786177/how-federal-disaster-money-favors-the-rich.

Kaba, Mariame. 2013. "Fifteen Things That We Relearned about the Prison Industrial Complex in 2013." *Truthout*, December 20, 2013. https://truthout.org/articles/fifteen-things-that-we-re-learned-about-the-prison-industrial-complex-in-2013/.

Lehmann, Evan, and Jean Chemnick. 2017. "Obama's Climate Legacy: 8 Years of Troubles and Triumphs." *E&E News*, January 20, 2017. https://www.eenews.net/stories/1060048703.

O'Neil, Lorena. 2016. "The Link between Natural Disasters and Domestic Abuse." *The Atlantic*, September 28, 2016. https://www.theatlantic.com/health/archive/2016/09/disaster-domestic-abuse/501299/.

Oxfam International. 2020. "Not All Gaps Are Created Equal: The True Value of Care Work." January 20, 2020. https://www.oxfam.org/en/not-all-gaps-are-created-equal-true-value-care-work.

Parkinson, Debra. 2019. "Investigating the Increase in Domestic Violence Post Disaster: An Australian Case Study." *Journal of Interpersonal Violence* 34 (11): 2333–2362. https://doi.org/10.1177/0886260517696876.

Royden, Amy. 2002. "US Climate Change Policy under President Clinton: A Look Back." *Golden Gate University Law Review* 32 (4): 415–478. https://digitalcommons.law.ggu.edu/ggulrev /vol32/iss4/3.

Rugh, Peter. 2013. "'Mi Lucha Es Tu Lucha'—Occupy Sandy's Collective Recovery." *Waging Nonviolence* (blog), February 1, 2013. https://wagingnonviolence.org/2013/02/mi-lucha-es-tu -lucha-occupy-sandys-collective-recovery/.

Thunberg, Greta. 2018. "The Disarming Case to Act Right Now on Climate Change." Filmed November 2018 in Sweden at TEDxStockholm. Video, 11:03. https://www.ted.com/talks/greta _thunberg_the_disarming_case_to_act_right_now_on_climate _change.

Vigaud-Walsh, Francisca. 2019. "Hurricane María's Survivors: 'Women's Safety Was Not Prioritized.'" *Refugees International*, September 13, 2019. https://reliefweb.int/report/puerto-rico -united-states-america/hurricane-mar-s-survivors-women-s -safety-was-not.

World Health Organization (WHO). 2005. "Violence and Disasters." https://web.archive.org/web/20051108033528/https://www .who.int/violence_injury_prevention/publications/violence /violence_disasters.pdf.

2

Slavery's Shadows

The Afterlife of Dispossession

MARISA J. FUENTES, CHRISTINA SHARPE,
AND MICHELLE COMMANDER

"If slavery persists as an issue in the political life of Black America," cultural historian Saidiya Hartman writes, "it is not because of an antiquarian obsession with bygone days or the burden of a too-long memory, but because Black lives are still imperiled and devalued by a racial calculus and a political arithmetic that were entrenched centuries ago. This is the afterlife of slavery—skewed life chances, limited access to health and education, premature death, incarceration, and impoverishment" (2007, 6). In March 2019, the Institute for Research on Women hosted a conversation with Marisa Fuentes and Christina Sharpe about how the traumatic experiences of slavery travel through time and space, affecting the study of the past as well as the present. Michelle Commander generously agreed to serve as a commentator. The following is an edited transcript of the event.

MARISA FUENTES: In Christina Sharpe's *In the Wake: On Blackness and Being* (2016), she describes, "Living with immi/a/nent death, in the shadow of that door, in the wake of slavery, with the obstructed passages of the Mediterranean, with carding, stop and frisk, the afterlives of partus sequitur ventrem, respiratory distress, detention centers, *Lagers*, prisons, and a multitude of other forms of surveillance" (132). Quoting Saidiya Hartman, she declares, "I want to do more than recount the violence that deposited these traces in the archive" (2008, 2, quoted in Sharpe 2016, 132). Sharpe continues, "I wanted to make present the someone that those eyes look out to. I wanted to stay in the wake to sound an ordinary note of care. I name it an ordinary note because it takes as weather the contemporary conditions of Black life and death" (132).

My first book, *Dispossessed Lives*, dwells on scenes of enslaved women's lives and deaths in the eighteenth-century Caribbean.[1] Sometime around Saturday, December 17, 1768, an enslaved woman named Molly living in Speightstown, Barbados, was executed. She was most likely hanged by the neck for an hour on an elevated wooden gallows built for that purpose or from a nearby tree to ensure a public spectacle. She was accused and condemned for attempting to poison John Denny, Esq., a member of the Barbados Council who was not her owner. Andrew Edwards, a local constable, was paid for apprehending her in the days before this moment and another slave likely pressed into service to assist in the execution. From the surviving archival fragments found in the Barbados Minutes of Council, we know that Molly would have looked down on a crowd of enslaved men and women gathered not only to bear witness to colonial brutality, but to take her body from the gallows and bury her in the ways of their community.

Like the silences surrounding other archival traces of enslaved women, we do not know which familial connections Molly left behind. The archive only documents what was meaningful to the governor's council, to her owner, and to the alleged victim in this case. This information included her name, monetary value, and the crime of which she was accused. Her owner, Isaac Wray, petitioned the council for compensation for the loss of his slave property, which was granted. Slave owners were paid 25 pounds from the colony's treasury for their executed slaves. We cannot know the circumstances leading up to Molly's conviction. The nullity of slave law makes it virtually impossible to defend oneself against such accusations. The enslaved community had a final chance to give Molly a voice, violating the sensibilities of white Barbadians. Our knowledge of the community's acts, however, depended upon chance. "As our present makes all too apparent," Saidiya Hartman reminds us, "there is no space outside the threat of death in which Black mourning can or could take place" (2016, 212).

What are the origins of "immi/a/nent [Black] death?" Where might we begin with our notice and care and to "make present" those whose lives and deaths were Blackness in excess? The hold. The transatlantic slave trade and its archive—a crucible of Black disposability—surfaces traces of discarded and disappearing lives. Saturating the records of the Royal African Company[2] are captives designated as "refuse slaves," who did not survive their American sale or who were sold for a trifle to speculators for being "almost dead."[3]

In the midst of my research for *Dispossessed Lives*, I was haunted by a document I can no longer find. A white man whose name I cannot remember petitioned the Barbados Council for a trifling amount of money. He requested payment for the cost of food he supplied to a captive African woman in a warehouse over the four days before she died. The woman was not named. The circumstance of her arrival in the Bridgetown warehouse was not information required by the Barbados Council. Someone carried her off a slave ship. She spent four days confined in another kind of hold, alone, without knowledge of her fate, without "an ordinary note of care" (Sharpe 2016, 132). After reading a century of execution records I found her in three lines of a routine petition for compensation—a recurring pattern of records in the logic of colonial administration that included applications from slave owners seeking compensation for their executed slaves. I had not imagined her. I remember her appearing in the archive even if I can no longer find the document or prove to anyone that she existed. I now ask the same rhetorical questions that emerged from *Dispossessed Lives*. What did her death mean to anyone on the ship, in the port, from her home? Did she refuse the food that the man brought? Who owned her or refused her? What did it mean for her to be in that warehouse alone but for a strange visitor and foreign food for four days? Who did she think of in her last moments?

I thought about this woman in the warehouse periodically, and she stayed with me through the writing of my first book. It was she, following Sarah Haley, who was dwelling with me. Or is it, as Yvette Christiansë (2006) describes, that the living long for the dead, that I came to haunt her? It is nonetheless this unnamed woman's archival trace in the accounting books of slavery that leads me to my next project on the African captives who were refused by slave owners, merchants, and traders in American slave-trading ports and who often perished in destination ports around the Atlantic world. One way to attend to these disposable lives is to consider the temporality of their last moments in life waiting in the hold or the pens and warehouses on shore. To pass on or over captive lives that ended during the slave trade is to reproduce archival erasure.

The historiography of the slave trade belies the unceasing repetition of captive deaths in these records: *Jamestown, Virginia, June 25, 1679*, a letter to England. "We received orders from Mr. Thomas [Thurloe] to take into our care the refuse Negroes for the Royal Africa Company and dispose of them as for the best we can. There were 14 in number, some of them so old, others so infirm that it is a shame that such Negroes should be shipped and aboard which serve only to annoy and destroy those of better value. There is two of them dead and two we believe will not live long."[4] *Barbados, May 8, 1709*, another report to investors: "11 they buried during the sale."[5] *Montserrat, April 26, 1712*, "50 Negroes from Barbados which proved very ordinary, seven died before sold any and several since."[6] *Antigua, June 15, 1714*, Mr. Edward Chester, Sr. writes that, "The eight slaves that the bill of mortality do not make out were left onboard the ship being not able to come over the side, the most of which are since dead, and the whole will not make out 40 pounds."[7]

Four days, a week or two at the end of a slave ship voyage across the Atlantic, make up the space between commodity and humanity, life and death. There was a kind of living in that temporal plane and a need to reckon with time. Accounting for these lives lost also provides us several pathways to ponder the status, value, and category or genre of human in the early modern Atlantic. Scholars in critical Black studies provide a theoretical language for deconstructing the universality of man from the human and open spaces. Alexander Weheliye (2014) argues for new objects of knowledge and tools to resist the naturalization of systems of racial, gender, and economic subjugation. I would argue that the archives of historical work on the slave trade and the category of "refuse slave" explicate a particular language of human liminality enmeshed within systems of economic violence. These archives push Black studies scholars back into the early modern era, into the wake of the slave trade, where concepts of race and susceptibility to death originally cohered for the project of white supremacy.

The challenge that *Dispossessed Lives* faced and this new project continues to confront is to write a history about what an archive does not offer, or to borrow from Christiansë, to write into "the space of a large silence" (2006, 350). The silence created through the brutal violence against enslaved people guided me to move toward particular methodologies that would enable me to think about the limits and possibilities of enslaved women's historical subjectivities. Molly, who was executed for allegedly poisoning a white man, symbolizes both the violence of slavery on bodies and the violence of the laws that prevented the enslaved from claims of humanity, of innocence. Jane, a fugitive from slavery, and the unnamed women in the final chapter of the book illuminate the manner in which mutilation, physical and epistemic, conditioned enslaved peoples' historicity, leading to questions about the impossibility of their recovery.

I endeavor to demonstrate how incomplete narratives, nonconforming structures, and different modes of writing can be used as tools to reveal a more tenable, ethical method to tell silent stories. Putting a single woman with a name, or a composite of women without names, at the center of a narrative forces a particular kind of attention on them. I wrote from a place that necessarily challenged the limited and terrifying language of documents and turned instead to how enslaved women might witness or represent their own circumstances even without a recognizable voice, by looking out at a scene or a heart-wrenching scream. This is another mode of historical writing that I hope gets us closer to attending to the devastation of slavery and offering a clearer understanding of the afterlives of slavery, and how violence continues to impact Black lives.

The nature of the archive from which enslaved people emerge requires this effort. We cannot redeem or rescue them, but we can consider their pain. My scholarship, in conversation with my colleagues here, has hewn to the dispossessed, the nameless, the violated Black lives in the era of Atlantic slavery. The enslaved women I attended to in *Dispossessed Lives* insisted upon my utilizing strategies to recount their experiences without replicating their violation or imposing imagined interiorities that they were not allowed to express in the archives. As Christina Sharpe reminds us, "For Black academics to produce legible work in the academy often means adhering to research methods that are 'drafted into the service of a larger, destructive force' . . . thereby doing violence to our own capacities to read, think, and imagine otherwise" (Sharpe 2016, 13). "We must become undisciplined," she continues. "The work we do requires new modes and methods of research and teaching, new ways of entering and leaving the archives of slavery, of undoing" (Sharpe 2016, 13), what Saidiya Hartman names "'the racial calculus and political arithmetic that were entrenched centuries ago'" (Hartman 2008, quoted in Sharpe 2016, 13).

The work of historical practice is risky. There is political risk in representing Black subjects in distress or succumbing to violence, and there is risk in the archival encounter in dwelling long with terror and violence. To sit with these sources and images, to be a witness, requires the capacity to hold and inhabit deep wells of pain and horror. One must persist for years in this mortuary of records to bring otherwise invisible lives to historical representation in a way that challenges the reproduction of invisibility and commodification. This process of living in the "weather" of anti-Blackness demands strategies to manage one's emotional responses to such brutality in order to persist with these subjects, to be willing to sit with this aspect of human degradation and to find meaning.

We have by now spent decades, centuries even, absorbing the brutalizations inflicted upon people of African descent and witnessing the processes by which humans cease to be. By reckoning unflinchingly with our methods and our ethical practices as scholars, our responsibility to our sources and subjects long dead, we might historically approximate what has typically been unrepresentable. This is a matter of not only reading along the bias grain, but also explicitly demonstrating how power works in making certain historical subjects invisible, brutally hyper-visible, and silent. This is an effort to reconstruct another kind of history that does not reproduce colonial and disciplinary power. I persist with this project not because it offers resolution or comfort in reconstructing lost Black lives.

This work insists that historical studies of the Black Atlantic inform the ways in which race, gender, and sexuality continue to shape the lives of African-descended people worldwide. These are histories of how Black people became disposable and objectified and vulnerable to the caprice, lusts, and economic desires of colonial authorities. This work documents the strategies and structures that made Black Atlantic lives subject to violence of thought and action. It offers material to reflect on the stakes of resistance in such systems and the reproduction of raced and gendered configu-rations of vulnerability. It begins to mark the way that the archive and history have erased Black bodies and how the legacies of slavery, the racialized sexism, and the legal, socioeconomic, and physical violence against people of African descent manifest in the violence that we continue to confront. It is a gesture toward a reckoning of our own time. It is a history of our present.

CHRISTINA SHARPE: I'll begin with a brief note about writing. I wrote *In the Wake* with a sense of urgency that has not abated in the two and a half years since the book was published. In

In the Wake, but also in my first book *Monstrous Intimacies: Making Post-Slavery Subjects*, especially in the introduction, I was trying to write out of and into a "we" that was Black and global and that recognized the phenomena that disproportionately and devastatingly affect Black people everywhere as the basis for theorizing and world-making. I was not interested in thinking about the non-Black desire to consume, produce, and stage spectacular and quotidian Black death. I thought it was enough for me to say that there is that desire and to establish it as the space from which we attempt to work.

The book activates multiple registers of "wake": as keeping watch over the dead, the track behind a moving ship, the consequence of awakening, and consciousness. It also activates multiple definitions of ship, cold, and weather. I weave together images, current catastrophes, and quotidian events and literature to understand the ways that slavery's still unresolved unfoldings are constitutive of the contemporary conditions of Black being in its spatial, legal, psychic, and material dimensions.

Central to the work are a number of ways I tried to theorize Black life through anagrammatical Blackness, practices of Black annotation and redaction, and "wake work," which speak to a range of experiences, refusals, and strategies. In each chapter, I try to position readers in ways of reading the past and the present archives of everyday violence so that we might approach Black being in the wake itself as consciousness, as thinking with and through the ongoing present of subjection and resistance as we attempt to imagine Black life anew.

I theorize the social, political, ecological ubiquity of anti-Blackness through "the weather," a concept that builds on Toni Morrison's formulation at the close of *Beloved*. I insist on the utility of "the weather" as a way for thinking and imagining livable Black presence and futures. "The weather" takes as fact the conjunction of anti-Blackness and white supremacy, a conjunction in which there seems to be agreement across political terrain and spectrums. White people not only sustain white supremacy but reproduce it and circulate it through the maintenance, production, and implementation of logics of innocence and guilt, a "brutal imagination" (a term that I borrow from Cornelius Eady's 2001 poetry collection *Brutal Imagination*) that produces anti-Black spaces and narratives that are always available, always present to be stepped into and animated.

My brief comments today are an attempt to attend to Black life that has been rendered disposable and ungrievable. My method here is one of thinking juxtapositionally; and it is in that spirit that I've attempted to place our works alongside each other. How does one approach the past when violence is the material? How does one approach such a past with care? I think that Marisa Fuentes's difficult and necessary book *Dispossessed Lives: Enslaved Women, Violence, and the Archive* provides one set of answers.

Fuentes takes us into the archives of slavery in eighteenth-century Barbados at a time when the majority of the population were women and where many of those women who were constituted as white claimed ownership over Black persons, many of whom were also women. In those archives, Fuentes encounters not so much the enslaved women themselves but the violence by which those enslaved and freed Black women were deposited there. It is an encounter with power, and Fuentes insists that we not forget that. In a 2017 conversation with Jennifer Morgan, author of *Laboring Women: Reproduction and Gender in New World Slavery*, Fuentes says that she wanted to understand how these enslaved women lived in such violation, lived in a "disempowerment so powerful that it traveled through time and affected . . . [our] ability to recreate any amount of their lives beyond the violence" ("Enslaved Women" 2017).

Saidiya Hartman in *Wayward Lives, Beautiful Experiments*, follows the early twentieth-century path of poor Black girls and women and stays with them, seeing and hearing them and bringing them close. Similarly, Fuentes in *Dispossessed Lives* refuses to accede to the archive of indifference, to the dead place where the worlds made by anti-Blackness and white supremacy would lodge these women. I believe that Fuentes has said that her method is guided by a refusal to surrender to the material outcome of the archive. In my own work I also want to attend to more than violence. I write that to be in the wake is to recognize the ways that we are "constituted through and by continued vulnerability to overwhelming force, though not *only* known to ourselves and to each other *by* that force" (2016, 16).

What, then, does such attention require? What are the methods necessary to attend to lives lived in relation to utter violence? What forms must one create or stretch, employ, adapt, and develop and recognize in order to attend to their lives—and to our lives—with care? What is required in order to open up a space to see and hear those enslaved and putatively free Black women and girls and boys and men who were interred in the archive or absented from it altogether? In my work, I wanted a form and a language that would allow Black people to live on the page and in the world. I have repeatedly read photographs and other visual and textual accounts that leave Black people in a register of abandonment, especially when they purport to produce something like empathy. I have tried to read and annotate and redact in order to bring into view the life that was already there.

Fuentes says that the Black women in the archives come to us, and we receive them in the condition of their violation. What does it mean to receive them, to admit or accept them, to give credit to them, to believe them, to admit a person to give evidence? I think that Fuentes shows us how to receive these Black women in and not only in their condition of abandoned violation. Fuentes enters these archives, and the Black women enter her text, and we enter her text, and her text enters and transforms us through her care and her methods.

In *Dispossessed Lives*, we begin with the geography of the body and the urban and other built environment, and the geography of punishment. The book centers enslaved Black women in their terrible encounters with power, and brings into view their struggles in the communities of enslaved people of which they were a part. Our movement through the book begins with an enslaved woman named Jane. We follow the path that Jane might have taken through Bridgetown on her fugitive flight. It is through this path that Fuentes takes us into the city to encounter "various spatial reminders of the looming violence of slavery" (Fuentes 2016, 21), and in particular, the technologies of control, surveillance, and punishment that helped constitute the urban environment and those who resided within it. Among those "reminders" are the cage, the crane, and the gallows, each a potential space for spectacular violence. When I first started reading *Dispossessed Lives*, I had to stop shortly afterwards. The description of the cage, an architecture of stunning cruelty and a movable torture chamber, stopped me. Originally designed as a site of punishment for sailors and indentured servants who had run away, it came to be reserved for fugitives from slavery.

In Letter IX from Crèvecoeur's *Letters from an American Farmer*, the narrator describes a brutalized, enslaved man, hanging in a cage, suspended from a tree, condemned to death by starvation for resisting enslavement. The narrator knows that the cage's placement, as terrible as he finds it, is not meant to terrorize him. Yet for the enslaved of Bridgetown, the terror of the cage and the cries of those enslaved people entombed alive in it, as many—and this is the description that stopped me—as many as 85 people in a space designed to hold at most 12, was a visual, sonic, and visceral lesson in terror and the consequences of refusal.

Like Fuentes, the Black Canadian historian Afua Cooper begins *The Hanging of Angélique* with geography. The narrator starts by walking through the old city of Montréal and the places that Marie-Joseph Angélique, an enslaved Black woman, would have moved through as she carried out and resisted the orders of those who claimed ownership over her. Marie-Joseph Angélique comes to Cooper through trial records. With both Fuentes's work and Cooper's, place enacts; the streets, which are still there, set a scene. In Barbados, the law dictated the manner and space where the punishment of enslaved people took place. Similarly, after being tried and found guilty of setting a fire that destroyed Montréal in New France in 1734, Marie-Joseph Angélique was tortured, and then placed on a cart that was moved through the city so that the enslaved and others might see her before she was hanged. Cooper suggests "that Angélique's geographies, the difference she made to the nation and Montréal spatially and philosophically, have created other spaces through which Black Canada can be articulated" (McKittrick 2006, xxx).

We have become accustomed to reading against the grain. But what Fuentes performs and proposes as method is reading along the bias grain. This method is first described in Fuentes's chapter on Agatha, where she reads for the Black women who do not appear. But it is a method she employs throughout the book.

Thinking with Fuentes, I was brought back to my first book, *Monstrous Intimacies*, and to questions of presumed/ assumed favor and power accruing to enslaved women through sexual relations, particularly with white men, who were oftentimes slave owners. I write about this in relation to Gayl Jones's novel *Corregidora* and the cases in Brazil in the

1870s brought against white women by enslaved women who charged that they were being prostituted. I also write about the question of sexual use in the introduction to *Monstrous Intimacies* in relation to Frederick Douglass's narrative representations of Aunt Hester. Here I write that Douglass captures the slave master's "violence, his pleasure, and the everyday tyranny of . . . life in slavery in which any white person (man, woman, or child) has the right to demand anything [from enslaved people]" (2010, 8).

Douglass positions Hester—I'm going to call her H/Esther because he rewrites Hester as Esther in 1855—"within an institution where 'every kitchen is a brothel,' every Black woman in the house or quarters a potential worker in it." Douglass positions Aunt H/Esther "in the midst of everyday intimate brutalities of white domestic domination, . . . within a psychic and material architectonics where there may be no escape from those brutalities but in the mind" (2010, 9). But if we stay with Douglass's words and Aunt H/Esther's scream, we are able to discern that H/Esther's desire for freedom is more than the violence that deposited her in the archive and in Douglass's text. In effect, what Douglass says is, for as long as I knew her, she suffered this thing, which I think we can read as for as long as I knew her, she insisted upon enacting her will in certain ways despite the cost.

In Fuentes's chapter on Venus, she writes, "Perhaps resistance to the violence of slavery," and I add to this the violence of slavery's wake and its afterlives, "is survival, the will to survive, the sound of someone wanting to be heard, wanting to live, or wanting to die. But the struggle against dehumanization is in the wanting. And sometimes we can hear it" (2016, 143). So I am going to circle back briefly to the beginning of our conversation. Guilty or not, Molly was executed. The care that her community took with her body, the esteem and regard that they showed her, so enraged and threatened the colonial authorities that they decreed that the bodies of executed enslaved people were henceforth to be weighted down with stones and dropped into the sea. Guilty or not, Marie-Joseph Angélique was tortured until she confessed. She was executed by hanging, her body burned, her ashes "flung to the four winds."

These were attempts to disprize beyond death. But in May 2018, at a police board meeting in Los Angeles, California, Sheila Hines-Brim threw the ashes of her niece, Wakiesha Wilson, who died in LAPD custody in 2016, at Charlie Beck, the head of the LAPD. As she threw them, she made the following powerful statement, "That's Wakiesha. She's going to stay with you." Hines-Brim was arrested, and after her release she said, "I used her ashes so they can be with him, so he can feel her, because he murdered her" (quoted in Da Silva 2018). Wakiesha Wilson's cries for help went unheard, or at least unattended to, in jail. I am not trying to decontextualize, or romanticize, or aestheticize Hines-Brim's act. I am trying to hear her. Hines-Brim's act is a refusal to not mourn and a refusal to not act in the face of murderous intent. Hines-Brim has taken the present into her own hands. We are both engaged in writing a history of the present, engaged in a reckoning with our own time.

MICHELLE COMMANDER: First, let me acknowledge Marisa and Christina for their wonderful and thought-provoking presentations.[8] I will begin with a stanza from Lucille Clifton's poem "i am accused of tending to the past" (2013).

> i am accused of tending to the past as if i made it,
> as if i sculpted it
> with my own hands. i did not.
> this past was waiting for me
> when I came, a monstrous unnamed baby.

How might we tend to the dead and the near dead, to those whose social alienation and dispossession are a bitter, spiritually engulfing inheritance?

As I have explored in my own work, people of African descent have attempted to establish a collective politics of refusal by assuming defiant postures in the imminence and eminence of death. That is, they have inaugurated standpoints for actively rejecting the ways that they are relegated to spaces and places that are proximate to death. I have discussed such creative employments of the imagination using the language of plays, reflecting across time and space on the ways that African diasporans have taken back control over their bodies, including those kidnapped and enslaved African peoples who resisted in literal and figurative ascension via rebellion during the Middle Passage by taking leaps from slave ships, aligning with one another to forge kinship networks, and via a long history of migration throughout the Atlantic world for presumably better chances at life.

In her book *In the Wake*, Christina Sharpe theorizes such intramural collective flights through the notion of "wake work," which she conceives of as a conceptual frame and location for Black people, to whom she dedicates the book, for imaginatively living otherwise paired with the principle of care, which relies not on the production of spectacular gestures but is very much inclusive of the quotidian. And by *quotidian*, here I mean mutual acknowledgement among Black peoples' recognition, commiseration, and sometimes just that prolonged sitting together to commune through and against precarity. Wake work is a mode of inhabiting and rupturing, in Sharpe's words, life in "the still unfolding aftermaths of . . . slavery" (Sharpe 2016, 2).

Though I've solely highlighted Sharpe's text here, I see this commitment in both of the commentaries shared today and in the labor exerted by these panelists to produce such a dynamic body of scholarship. As Fuentes and Sharpe's writings demonstrate, doing this kind of literary archeology, historical fabulation, and speculative work in slavery's afterlife involves capturing the myriad ways that Black people have creatively traversed the wildernesses that are ostensibly "post"—such as post-slavery, post-colonialism—and have endeavored to live despite everyday reminders of the bleakness under and in which they languish. Such efforts to take care are the collective movement away from a hovering over imaginatively and a steadfast commitment to loosening oneself into others, including those lost to history, from the merciless mire.

That is not to say that maintaining such a posture is easy. We all have stories about the toll it takes to confront the breadth of the losses that are announced by the archive. In *Lose Your Mother*, Saidiya Hartman writes about doing this kind of work in slavery's shadows. And here in this quote that I am about to read, she is reflecting on her attempt at simultaneously conducting scholarly research as well as dealing with a lot of the personal questions that she has about living in diaspora. She writes:

> Reckoning with my inheritance had driven me to the dungeon, but now it all seemed elusive. I struggled to connect the thoughts between then and now and to chart the trajectory between the goalpost in Curaçao and Montgomery and Brooklyn, but I kept fumbling.
>
> I could rattle off all the arguments about the devastating effects of having been property, denied the protection of citizenship, and stripped of rights of equality. The simple fact was that we still lived in a world in which racism sorts the haves and the have-nots and decides who lives and who dies. . . . This in part explained why I was in the dungeon, but it was personal, too. Hovering in an empty room was my attempt to figure out how this underground had created and marked me. (2008, 129)

I have a series of questions which I hope that our panelists and you, our audience, will engage with. As historians, poets, cultural producers, and cultural studies scholars—I hope I've gotten everybody here—what are we to make of archival silences and gaps? How do we narrate histories whose plots, characters, and narrative arcs, twists, and contradictions are not captured in physical sources but in traces and absences? What are the ethical implications of doing archival speculation? I would love if you would say more about your posture in conducting research in slavery's archive. [A related question is], what are the limitations of conceptualizing our moment as part of slavery's afterlife? I was thinking about the confines of discipline and especially about how historians have reacted to a new methodology and thinking about this afterlife, the temporality of things. But I was also thinking about the ways in which you, Marisa, and also Christina, fall into the first person in your text, which goes against a lot of traditions of discipline. So you may address any part of those questions as you wish.

MARISA FUENTES: I was writing in a field—histories of slavery—where the narrative of resistance was very dominant. I retrospectively understand why. It is really hard to sit with this type of archive and these types of defeats. When it comes to thinking about method, the way I approach these archives and these women, and the historical violence in which they were encapsulated, is to do no harm. I learned from amazing scholars to really pay attention to vulnerability and people in danger. I wrote to make sure that we were not numb to the violence. At the same time, I tried not to gratuitously reproduce it. That is really hard and I don't know that I have succeeded—I don't know if anyone could succeed at that. But I certainly took to heart Hartman's caution that if you are writing about slavery and you are writing about forms of violence, you are inevitably reproducing that.

How can we engage this inevitability without doing more harm? The posture that I took was speaking about ethics. Christina and I were writing these books at the same time. I did not know her. Yet we came to the same sense of urgency about doing no harm and the importance of documenting and attending to the lives of Black people in peril.

There's a way in which this is a second book because it is so risky and undisciplined. People say that you break the fourth wall as a historian by talking about how one writes or thinks about the archive. I was so self-conscious that I purposely did not put "I" into the text until the epilogue, which was the safe space to do it. I felt that there needed to be an epilogue to reflect on method and encounter and how we are placed sitting with this material and these images.

How have historians reacted? Surprisingly well. But this is after Saidiya Hartman's *Scenes of Subjection*. This is after Jennifer Morgan's *Laboring Women*. This is after Deborah Gray White's *Ar'n't I a Woman?* And this is after multitudes of Black feminist texts demanded this work of historians. It was in *that* wake. It was that historians were ready to receive this text in a way they might not have been 10 or 15 years ago.

CHRISTINA SHARPE: I would agree with Marisa, to say that first it is important to try to do no additional harm. There are moments where I was really conscious that I had to take care in reading images and reproducing accounts of violence.

I don't work in the archives in the same way as Marisa, but there are images that I read, and read, and reread in *In the Wake* because I was looking for more than the ways in which the images come to us in the aftermath of disaster. They are meant to produce a kind of empathy, but they don't. Instead, they frequently work to confirm the position of Black people as abandoned, grotesque. In *Monstrous Intimacies*, I quote Jesse Jackson, who describes the great appetite for the production and circulation of Black suffering.

I was most anxious about the first fifteen pages of *In the Wake*, where I use the autobiographical "I." It wasn't because of disciplinary concerns but about subjecting my family to particular kinds of scrutiny, particularly without their permission. There are moments where I say, "That's not my story to tell."

[You may have heard] in the news recently about the woman who is suing Harvard about the daguerreotypes of Delia and Renty [two enslaved people who are her ancestors]. I first wrote about those daguerreotypes in *Monstrous Intimacies*, and I thought about reproducing them but decided against it. I didn't give them a sustained enough reading to warrant their inclusion, and what would I be reproducing if I used them? I returned to the daguerreotypes in *In the Wake*, and reproduced just a strip of Delia and Drana's eyes to refocus on what they might be seeing when they look out and across time to us.

My posture was one of refusing to occupy a particular notion of objectivity. Whether I included the personal "I" or not, that personal "I" would have informed every aspect of this book, especially in the midst of personal losses. I tried very hard not to leave Black people in a register of abandonment. I tried to theorize and to see the ways in which we may be constituted through vulnerability. But that's not the only way we see each other. That's not our only way of being in the world.

MARISA FUENTES: I just wanted to follow up on something you said. We both talk about what we do methodologically. We are trying—and your language is stunning—"not to leave Black people in a register of abandonment." But I'm wondering if you could talk a little bit about the specificity of method in redaction and annotation and why you chose to read, and be in conversation with, and witness those images.

CHRISTINA SHARPE: That's a great question. I was thinking about a variety of ways by which we come to understand and elaborate our own lives. As I said today, I think juxtaposition-ally. I am writing in the midst of report after report after report of Black people being murdered by the police, and in the wake of my own cousin being murdered by the police years before.

I started to think about the second autopsy that Michael Brown's parents paid for in order to prove injury, and the ways that it would and wouldn't help them. What might we think of as an annotation or redaction employed by Black people that would not look to convince others, but that was an acknowledgment of being and the ways in which we had been violated? Those annotations worked for this family, and they worked for many Black people, but they didn't work to convince anyone else, or the state, that Michael Brown was not the author of his own violent death.

What about you, in terms of method, and your new project on refuse slaves? One of the things I always say to people when I recommend Marisa's work is, "It is extraordinary, and I don't know how she did it." I am so happy that in the epilogue to *Dispossessed Lives* you talk about the cost of sitting with such violence all the time. My students often ask me, "How did you do it?" I want to talk about method: it has a cost, but also an ethical charge because of the violence that was done to these women. It is taking up an ethical charge to sit with them.

MARISA FUENTES: I think method is crucial to navigating power and unrelenting violent representation. The end of the book was the hardest part to write because the women experienced such spectacular violence. I thought of a way to raise questions that would let us see what the archive would never let us see: what violence does to the body and how you survive violence. It isn't just, "Oh, I survived." You actually carry the marks and the injuries for the rest of your life. What is it like to then live with injury? I'm thinking of ways to enter these stories again without reproducing violation.

I remain interested in searching for and sitting with people who had no chance. The "refuse slaves" are always left out because they are the ones who died. There's nothing to say because they are the ones thrown overboard. We know they count as a number, as an addendum to the people who survived the Middle Passage and lived their lives in slavery. They are all over the archive. We need to stop and pause and think. Temporality becomes another method. What seem to us to be short moments actually mark the end of somebody's life.

I get the question from students: "How does it affect you? How do you take care of yourself?" I usually conjure up the image of a trauma surgeon, somebody who has the capacity day in and day out to attend to human life in its most vulnerable form. I couldn't do that. That is not my work at all. But for some reason I can do this. It is not easy at all, and you do have to stop and put it down, walk out of the door, do something else, distract yourself so that your mind can have a rest. What makes it even more difficult is that we continue to live in a state of emergency.

CHRISTINA SHARPE: That is the thing. You don't just peruse those records and then walk out into the world, where they cease to exist. We're still living through their production.

Notes

1. Portions of the transcribed presentation are reproduced from *Dispossessed Lives*. See Fuentes 2016, 101, 146–148. This discussion was part of the Institute for Research on Women's Distinguished Lecture Series in which the authors shared excerpts and ideas from recent publications.

2. The Royal African Company held a monopoly of the British slave trade between 1672 and 1731. See Law 2004.

3. The Invoice Book Homewards of the Royal African Company of England, No. H 1 from August 29, 1673, to February 24, 1676. Barbados, August 4, 1674, T70/936/1, 32, The National Archives of the UK, Kew, London (hereafter referred to as TNA).

4. Letter from Mr. Nathaniel Bacon & Mr. Edward Jones to Royal African Company Merchants, June 25, 1679, T70/1, 13, TNA, Kew, London.

5. Letter from Mr. Raynes, Bate & Thomas Stewart to RAC, May 9, 1709, T70/2, 9/13, TNA.

6. Letter from Mr. William Frye to RAC, April 26, 1712, T70/2, 42, TNA.

7. Letter from Mr. Edward Chester to RAC, June 15, 1714, T70/3, 48/32, TNA.

8. Portions of these remarks are reproduced from Commander 2018.

References

Christiansë, Yvette. 2006. *Unconfessed*. New York: Other Press.

Clifton, Lucille. 2013. "i am accused of tending to the past." *Reflections* (Spring 2013). https://reflections.yale.edu/article/future-race/i-am-accused-tending-past.

Commander, Michelle. 2018. "Poetics and Care in the Wake." *ASAP/Journal* 3, no. 2: 310–314.

Cooper, Afua. 2007. *The Hanging of Angélique: The Untold Story of Canadian Slavery and the Burning of Old Montréal*. Athens: University of Georgia Press.

Crèvecoeur, Jean de. (1782) 2007. *Letters from an American Farmer*. Reprint, Carlisle, MA: Applewood Books.

Da Silva, Chantal. 2018. "Ashes of Woman Who Died in Police Custody Thrown at LAPD Chief." *Newsweek*, May 9, 2018. https://www.newsweek.com/ashes-woman-who-died-police -custody-thrown-lapd-chief-916501.

"Enslaved Women and the Ethical Practice of History, A Conversa- tion between Marisa J. Fuentes and Jennifer L. Morgan." 2017. Lapidus Center for the Historical Analysis of Transatlantic Slavery at the Schomburg Center for Research in Black Culture, New York City. March 7, 2017. Video, 1:24:47. https://livestream .com/schomburgcenter/events/6987875/videos/151206685.

Fuentes, Marisa, J. 2016. *Dispossessed Lives: Enslaved Women, Violence, and the Archive*. Philadelphia: University of Pennsylva- nia Press.

Hartman, Saidiya, V. 1997. *Scenes of Subjection: Terror, Slavery, and Self-Making in Nineteenth-Century America*. New York: Oxford University Press.

———. 2007. *Lose Your Mother: A Journey along the Atlantic Slave Route*. New York: Farrar, Straus and Giroux.

———. 2008. "Venus in Two Acts." *Small Axe* 26, 1–14.

———. 2016. "The Dead Book Revisited." *History of the Present: A Journal of Critical History* 6, no. 2 (Fall): 208–215.

———. 2019. *Wayward Lives, Beautiful Experiments: Intimate Histories of Riotous Black Girls, Troublesome Women, and Queer Radicals*. New York: W. W. Norton.

Jones, Gayl. (1975) 1987. *Corregidora*. Reprint, Boston, MA: Beacon Press.

Law, Robin. 2004. *Ouidah: The Social History of a West African Slaving "Port," 1727–1892*. Athens: Ohio University Press.

McKittrick, Katherine. 2006. *Demonic Grounds: Black Women and the Cartographies of Struggle*. Minneapolis: University of Minnesota Press.

Morgan, Jennifer L. 2004. *Laboring Women: Gender and Reproduction in the Making of New World Slavery*. Philadelphia: University of Pennsylvania Press.

Sharpe, Christina. 2010. *Monstrous Intimacies: Making Post-Slavery Subjects*. Durham, NC: Duke University Press.

———. 2016. *In the Wake: On Blackness and Being*. Durham, NC: Duke University Press.

Weheliye, Alexander. 2014. *Habeas Viscus: Racializing Assemblages, Biopolitics, and Black Feminist Theories of the Human*. Durham, NC: Duke University Press.

White, Deborah Gray. 1985. *Ar'n't I a Woman? Female Slaves in the Plantation South*. New York: W. W. Norton.

3

The Cruelty Is the Point

Women and Children as Weapons in the War on Drugs

JENNIFER FLYNN WALKER AND
BELA AUGUST WALKER

I never used any drugs in front of my children. My landlord called
CPS to get me evicted. He told me he would. I thought if I asked
for help with my addiction, I would get it. The caseworker told
me that I would get it. She lied and now I'm in hell. My kids are in
Indiana in foster care and I can't afford to see them and if I don't
see them, I will lose them. They are mad at me. I couldn't save
them from being taken. I live in hell. Honestly, I think it would
have been better if I overdosed.
—Di from Ohio

Long before the COVID-19 pandemic, our country was in
the midst of a different kind of public health emergency. The
opioid epidemic, which encompasses prescription and illegal opioids, as well as other misused drugs, has far-reaching
consequences. Every day, over two hundred people in the
United States die from opioid overdose (CDC 2022).[1] Each
year, more people in the United States perish from drug overdose than died during the Vietnam War. These figures
increased over the past decade (Hedegaard et al. 2020) and

accelerated during the coronavirus pandemic (CDC 2022). This latest phase of "addiction trajectory"—to borrow and modify a term coined by anthropologists Eugene Raikhel and William Garriott (2013)—continues decades of intentional criminalization of drug use as a means to maintain an underclass in the United States.

While this country suffers through the impact of opioid dependence, our solutions have been at best substandard and at worst cruel. Governmental responses, often erratic and ineffective, have exacerbated the crisis. Communities devastated by the collateral consequences of criminalizing drugs demand action. In response, politicians offer increased criminal penalties and over-policing. These policies are not successful in protecting communities from harm or families from losing loved ones to overdose. Yet, the way forward is blindingly simple. Scientific research has consistently proven that a medical approach, combined with increased access to drug treatment, most effectively and economically treats addiction. Despite this evidence, governments have devoted sparse resources to harm reduction treatment. Rather than expanding access to meet growing needs, state and federal governments have limited funds for proven treatment options like medication-assisted treatment, syringe access programs, and low-threshold harm reduction programs.

Instead of therapeutic responses to addiction, governments have resorted to punishing people who use drugs. Many scholars have described the devastating effects of incarceration on people with addictions, their families, and their communities. The current War on Drugs, which began in the 1970s, encompasses government policies designed to stop illegal drug use and distribution by dramatically increasing prison sentences for both drug dealers and users. As a "war," its tactics focus on punishment, rather than effective ways to protect a community and make it healthier. The War on Drugs has devastated Black and Brown communities. Black men have been sent to prison for drug-related crimes at a staggering rate (Haney and Zimbardo 1998). This war has also disproportionately impacted women, particularly Black women (Ritchie 2017).

Perhaps the most devastating of all tactics in the War on Drugs is the punitive use of the child welfare system. Like mass incarceration, the child welfare system has become a form of social control and racial oppression, destroying families and communities under the guise of helping them (Roberts 2002, 2022). Within the context of the opioid epidemic, a system ostensibly created to protect children almost universally harms them. The child welfare system gives state actors unprecedented authority to surveil any family and potentially sever the parent-child relationship—one of the most traumatic actions the state can commit. In this way, the child welfare system serves as an extension of our flawed system of over-policing (Roberts 2022). Such governmental forces operate without the scrutiny of lawmakers and outside of formal legal proceedings. Until states constrict their extra-judicial tactics, we will continue to place families in danger and scapegoat people affected by opioid addiction, who need government services. As sociologist Alex Vitale has demonstrated, "[t]he problem is not police training, police diversity, or police methods. . . . The problem is policing itself" (2017, cover copy). Child Protective Services (CPS) can't be reformed. We add our voices to those calling for the abolition of CPS as we know it.

Examining the Opioid Epidemic

Drug overdoses are a leading cause of death in the United States. Over two-thirds of these deaths involve opioids

(Wilson et al. 2020). In comparison to other modern drug epidemics, however, private business played a unique role in fueling the rise of opioid addiction. The modern opioid epidemic exploded in the mid 1990s through a combination of overzealous pharmaceutical companies and government inaction. During the late nineteenth century, as many as one out of two hundred Americans was addicted to opiates (Trickey 2018; Courtwright 2001). This number decreased at the beginning of the twentieth century, brought down, at least in part, by a change in medical prescribing practice (Courtwright 2001). Close to a century later, in 1996, Purdue Pharma introduced OxyContin to the public, changing the landscape of opioid addiction forever. More than simply producing this new drug, Purdue Pharma, led by the Sackler family, aggressively marketed OxyContin to physicians and the public, spending millions on advertising and making billions in the process (Van Zee 2009). Purdue encouraged widespread use of the drug, spotlighting its supposed nonaddictive nature, despite their own studies to the contrary (Keefe 2017). In 1996, the FDA approved Purdue marketing materials asserting that addiction occurrence was "very rare" (Van Zee 2009, 224). While OxyContin surged in popularity, government regulators remained silent (Lexchin and Kohler 2011; Noah 2019). Those states with more rigorous regulation (in particular, the use of triplicate prescription programs) had substantial reductions in distribution of OxyContin and subsequent overdose deaths (Alpert et al. 2022), but for the most part, the government crackdown came too late to stem the tide of addiction.

In contrast to other drug epidemics, the opioid epidemic has been painted white. Throughout U.S. history, drug users have always been predominantly white, but drug scares have often been framed in relation to people of color. In response, crackdowns have been violent and punitive. Despite similar rates of drug use, African Americans have been "6–10 times more likely to be incarcerated for drug offenses" (Netherland and Hansen 2017, 217). Since the beginning of the opioid epidemic, African Americans have had lower rates of opioid misuse, due in part to racial biases in prescribing prescription opioids (Alexander et al. 2018). While the gap is decreasing (Furr-Holden et al. 2021), the media stereotype of the opioid user remains focused on "sympathetic portrayals of suburban white prescription opioid users"—in contrast to "criminalized urban black and Latino heroin injectors" (Netherland and Hansen 2016, 664). The political rhetoric of the crisis has shifted as well: instead of solely a criminal justice issue, people have begun to discuss the opioid epidemic as an urgent public health matter (Om 2018).

The War on Drugs and Disproportionate Harm

In 2016, reporter Dan Baum tracked down Nixon policy advisor John Ehrlichman to ask him how the United States became entangled in the War on Drugs. Ehrlichman spelled out the clear connection between racism and government drug policy.

> "You want to know what this was really all about?" [Ehlichman] asked with the bluntness of a man who, after public disgrace and a stretch in federal prison, had little left to protect. "The Nixon campaign in 1968, and the Nixon White House after that, had two enemies: the antiwar left and black people. . . . We knew we couldn't make it illegal to be either against the war or black, but by getting the public to associate the hippies with marijuana and blacks with heroin,

and then criminalizing both heavily, we could disrupt those communities. We could arrest their leaders, raid their homes, break up their meetings, and vilify them night after night on the evening news. Did we know we were lying about the drugs? Of course we did." (quoted in Baum 2016)

The War on Drugs, beginning in the 1970s, led to harsh sentencing laws and mandatory minimum sentences for drug offenses, which has resulted in a significant increase in the number of people incarcerated for drug offenses (Alexander 2010). Black Americans are more likely to be arrested, prosecuted, and sentenced to longer prison terms for drug offenses than white Americans, despite similar rates of drug use (Alexander 2010). The United States has sent African American men to prison at a rate approximately four times the rate of incarceration of Black men in South Africa under apartheid (Haney and Zimbardo 1998). The number of Black men in prison in the United States has surpassed the number of enslaved men at the height of slavery (Alexander 2010). Black and Brown individuals are often perceived as more violent and dangerous than white individuals, leading to harsher sentencing and more punitive policies (Alexander 2010). By disproportionately targeting communities of color, who now constitute over 60 percent of those behind bars, the prison system in the United States perpetuates white supremacy (Carson 2022).

The War on Drugs also disproportionately affects women. For centuries, opiates were considered a "woman's drug" (Hager 2019, 49). Beginning in the nineteenth century, while alcohol and tobacco were considered male pursuits, doctors recommended opioids as a socially acceptable treatment for women; they were used to treat everything from "hysteria" to childbirth (Hager 2019). The drugs were prescribed liberally: "Up through the turn of the century, morphine was a literal prescription for bourgeois femininity" (Keire 1998, 809). Consequently, the face of the epidemic at the turn of the twentieth century was also female, personified by "genteel, southern, White, upper-middle class women" (Kandall 2010, 119). Statistics support this image, as two-thirds of those addicted to opioids at this time were female (Terplan 2017). The numbers began to change in the early 1900s, particularly after federal and state law discouraged opioid prescriptions and iatrogenic addiction (addiction by people using opioids under medical supervision) waned (Courtwright 2001). In the first half of the twentieth century, the image of the opiate addict shifted to "a young man of the urban lower classes who had originally experimented with drugs for pleasure" (Keire 1998, 809).

Now the pendulum has swung back. Once more, "[w]omen, particularly white reproductive-age women, are increasingly the face of the opioid crisis" (Terplan 2017, 195). Once again, addiction under medical supervision drives this gender divide, with doctors being twice as likely to prescribe opioids for women than for men, especially for chronic pain, such as back pain or migraines (Serdarevic et al. 2017). Studies show that women are prescribed opioids more frequently and in higher doses than men, despite experiencing pain at similar levels (Mojtabai et al. 2019). African Americans continue to be undertreated for pain and are less likely to receive opioid prescriptions than white individuals (Hoffman et al. 2016), a discriminatory practice dating back to the American Civil War (Jones 2021); when clinicians do prescribe opioids to African Americans, they assign lower doses than those given to white patients (Morden et al. 2021). Once addicted, women encounter high barriers to treatment. Mothers, in particular, suffer from logistical challenges and enhanced stigmatization (Lamonica and Boeri 2020). Many methadone clinics deny access to women who are pregnant, despite methadone treatment being the recommended standard of care for pregnant women who use opioids (Radel et al. 2018).

Women are more than twice as likely to be incarcerated for drug crimes as men and constitute the fastest-growing population in U.S. prisons, with almost 30 percent incarcerated for nonviolent drug offenses (Beall 2018; Carson 2022; Provance 2022). This number is disproportionately comprised of people of color—African American, Latinx, and Native American (Carson 2022)—and drug arrests have fueled this racial disparity (Harmon and Boppre 2018). Black women, in particular, are "the largest growing subgroup of those incarcerated," an increase spurred on by low-level drug offenses (Harmon and Boppre 2018, 310, 328).[2]

Women are also disproportionately affected by the collateral consequences of drug policies, including the loss of child custody, housing, and employment opportunities (Lenox 2011). Women who use drugs or have a history of drug use are often denied custody of their children, even if they are not deemed to be unfit parents (Lenox 2011). Women who have drug-related criminal records also face barriers to accessing housing and employment, making it difficult for them to reintegrate into society after serving their sentences (Lenox 2011). Women who use opioids are also at higher risk for domestic violence and other forms of abuse, which can further exacerbate their health and social problems (Mazure and Fiellin 2018).

The Child Welfare System and White Supremacy

The purpose of the Child Protective Services (CPS) system in the United States is to protect children from abuse and neglect, but it is built on a foundation of white supremacy that has resulted in disproportionate harm to communities of color. In the same way that racism is deeply rooted in every facet of American life, its legacy is embedded in the structure of our laws and our social system, which invariably includes the state's response to parent-child relationships. Removing children from their families has served as a means of social control for centuries. During slavery, the unilateral ability to sever families served as a powerful tool for slave owners. This destruction of African American families in the American South continued well after slavery through civil and criminal laws that recreated a system of forced labor (Blackmon 2008). At the beginning of the nineteenth century, immigrants from "undesirable" ethnic groups might find their children placed on orphan trains destined for "superior" families in the West and frequently used as forced labor in their new homes (Bates 2016). Similarly, the story of Native American separation through boarding schools is well known. Despite the eventual dissolution of the boarding school system and legal interventions like the Indian Child Welfare Act, state-sanctioned disruption of Native families has continued (Graham 2001).

The legacy of family separation continues today. The foster care system disproportionately targets people of color, particularly African Americans (Puzzanchera and Taylor 2020; NCJFCJ 2017; Center for the Study of Social Policy 2011). Children of color are more likely to be removed from their homes and placed in foster care than white children, even when they are not at higher risk of abuse or neglect. This racial bias in the CPS system is harmful to families and perpetuates racial inequities.

Black women in particular are viewed as less competent parents. Their families are seen as less deserving of protection or privacy (Walker 2008).[3] The smaller the proportion of African Americans in a particular community, the more likely they are to be targeted by child welfare systems (Freisthler et al. 2007; Garland et al. 1998; Maguire-Jack et al. 2020). The disparities are stark: between 2000 and 2011, "15.4% of Native American and 11.5% of African American children were likely to be placed in foster care before age 18 (compared to 5.4% of Hispanics, 4.9% of Whites, and 2.1% of Asians)" (Stephens et al. 2020). Currently, African American children constitute 23 percent of youth in foster care, despite representing only 14 percent of the U.S. population as a whole (Dettlaff and Boyd 2020, 253–254).[4] By the time they are eighteen, over 50 percent of Black children will have been subject to a child welfare investigation (Roberts 2021).

In theory, the legal sphere of privacy is rightly breached by child welfare systems to provide aid to minors otherwise unable to help themselves. In practice, the intrusion has been applied erratically and inequitably. White upper- and middle-class families are rarely disrupted by the state, regardless of what occurs inside them. On the other hand, groups traditionally subject to governmental scrutiny—typically the poor and racialized minorities—have found their domestic lives subject to state intrusion and even destruction. Families who ask the state for assistance often lose their privacy rights in the process (Bridges 2017); their lives become subject to scrutiny and micromanagement.

CPS has a history of removing children from their families without sufficient evidence of abuse or even neglect, placing them in situations that are just as dangerous as their previous circumstances, if not more. The system can be arbitrary and biased, with decisions made based on factors such as race, socioeconomic status, and other demographic factors. Significantly, nearly every decision in the Child Protective Services system takes place outside of a courtroom. From the beginning, a simple anonymous phone call sets off a mandatory visit from a CPS caseworker. These employees typically are not skilled social workers and only received basic on-the-job training.

The case manager holds incredible power. They can decide that a person is an unfit parent because their home is messy, or their clothes look unkempt. They can decide that a household's vegetarian diet is unhealthy, even if doctors disagree. Caseworkers often make the assumption that parents who use drugs, or who are suspected of using drugs or are in a relationship with someone who uses drugs, are unable to care for a child, even without evidence of actual abuse (Brewington 2022). As a result, children of people who use drugs are often removed from parental custody, and "case plans are frequently created without solid clinical information about substance use or other important factors" (Radel et al. 2018, 6). Parents have little recourse, because judges are only involved when the agency has made a determination to sever familial relationships, and at this point it is often too difficult to make a clear case to the contrary. The judge typically favors Child Protective Services.

Our current child welfare system resulted from the Adoption and Safe Families Act of 1997 (ASFA). ASFA transformed the primary goal of the child welfare system from reuniting families to "protecting" children.[5] The act facilitates the termination of parental rights, creating a fast track to adoption intended to alleviate the overburdened foster care system. The most sweeping legal change requires states to move to terminate parental rights for children who have been in foster care for fifteen out of the last twenty-two months. While the passage of the Family First Prevention Services Act in 2018 ostensibly aimed to increase family reunification services, its impact has been minimal (Trivedi 2022). Additionally, financial incentives continue to drive foster care, with agencies receiving more funding for each child they remove from a home (Roberts 2022).

The system's overreach is unprecedented and continues to expand. According to a ten-year study by the American Public Health Association, an alarming 37.4 percent of all children experience a Child Protective Services investigation before they are eighteen years old (Kim et al. 2017). Based on current census data, this amounts to 27.7 million children (Kim et al. 2017). Moreover, CPS policies and practices are often based on white middle-class norms, which are not necessarily applicable to families from different cultural backgrounds. For example, CPS may prioritize individualism and autonomy in child-rearing, while many families of color prioritize interdependence and communalism (Roberts 2022). This cultural mismatch can lead to misunderstandings and conflicts between CPS workers and families, which result in unnecessary removal of children from their homes. Additionally, white observers tend to view Black parents as more neglectful and abusive than white parents, even when their behaviors are identical (Roberts 2022). This implicit bias can influence the CPS workers' assessment of the situation and lead to disproportionate removal of children from families of color.

The disproportionate removal of children from families of color has devastating consequences for both children and parents. The forceful, immediate removal of a parent from their child's life causes lifelong scars. Even the most loving foster care environments prove disruptive. Children who are placed in foster care are more likely to experience instability and trauma, and are less likely to graduate from high school or attend college (Wildeman and Emanuel 2014). Parents who have their children removed from their homes may experience shame, loss, and trauma, which can interfere with their ability to provide a safe and stable home for their children in the future (Roberts 2022). Ideally, separating children from their parents should only occur in the most severe of situations. Instead, foster care has become a booming business due to the government's use of the child welfare system as a mechanism to surveil and punish people who use drugs.

Policy Approaches to the Opioid Epidemic

Drug policies in the United States have historically been based on a criminal justice approach, with punitive measures being the primary response to drug use and addiction. The harshest of these punishments has been to destroy families, first by removing Black men through giving them long prison sentences and subsequently by removing children and placing them into mostly white homes or into for-profit foster care. However, this approach has proven to be ineffective and harmful, particularly for Black and Brown communities. It is time to view drug policies through a public health lens, recognizing substance use disorder as a complex health issue rather than criminal behavior.

Substance use disorder is a health issue that requires treatment and support rather than punishment. Addiction is a chronic brain disease that alters the brain's reward system, making it difficult for individuals to control their drug use (NIDA 2021). Punitive measures, such as incarceration, do not address the underlying causes of addiction and may exacerbate the problem by creating more stress and trauma for individuals who are already struggling (Cohen et al. 2022). A public health approach, on the other hand, recognizes addiction as a treatable condition and focuses on providing access to evidence-based treatment and support services.

Drug addiction is often linked to other health and social issues, such as poverty, homelessness, and mental illness.

Substance use disorders are typically associated with economic hardship. Opioid use rises with unemployment (Azagba et al. 2021; Matthews et al. 2022). Additionally, unemployment and opioid overdoses and deaths are directly correlated (da Costa 2017). In the United States, for every 1 percentage point the unemployment rate increases, the opioid death rate per 100,000 rises by 0.19 (3.6 percent) and the opioid overdose emergency department visit rate per 100,000 increases by 0.95 (7.0 percent) (NBER 2017). Homelessness spurs higher rates of opioid addiction and overdose (Milaney et al. 2021; Yamamoto et al. 2019). Punitive drug policies do not address these underlying issues and may even worsen them by disrupting families and communities (Cohen et al. 2022). A public health approach, on the other hand, recognizes the interconnectedness of health and social issues and focuses on addressing these underlying issues through a comprehensive, integrated approach that includes access to healthcare, housing, and social services.

A public health approach to drug policy has been shown to be more effective in reducing drug-related harm than a criminal justice approach. In Portugal, for example, drug possession for personal use was decriminalized in 2001, and drug addiction was recognized as a health issue rather than a criminal behavior (Hughes and Stevens 2012). As a result, Portugal has seen a significant reduction in drug-related harms, including HIV infections, overdose deaths, and drug-related crime. The decriminalization of drug possession for personal use has also allowed for more resources to be allocated to prevention, treatment, and harm reduction services, which has contributed to further reductions in drug-related harms (Hughes and Stevens 2012). A public health approach that includes access to evidence-based treatment, harm reduction services, and overdose prevention measures has been shown to be more effective in reducing overdose deaths as well as more economically efficient (Fairley et al. 2021; Kolodny et al. 2015).

The U.S. criminal justice approach to drug policy has failed to stem the opioid epidemic. Punitive measures, such as increased law enforcement efforts and harsher sentencing for drug offenses, have not been effective in reducing the number of overdose deaths (Kolodny et al. 2015). Scientific research has consistently proven that a medical approach combined with increased access to drug treatment most successfully and economically treats drug addiction (Mojtabai et al. 2019; Wakeman 2016; Wiercigroch et al. 2020). Studies show that substance use disorder can most effectively be treated with prescription buprenorphine, or other medication-assisted treatment (MAT) (Connery 2015; ICER 2014; Wakeman 2016). While doctors can prescribe opioids or morphine without any barriers, they may not prescribe bupenorphine until they complete additional training, a requirement unique to this medication (Nunes et al. 2021). Doctors treating patients with bupenorphine must also mandate frequent in-person visits (Nunes et al. 2021). When COVID-19 hit, some of the restrictions on prescribing buprenorphine were lifted out of necessity (Luigi et al. 2021; Samuels et al. 2020; Wang et al. 2021). Subsequent studies have demonstrated that lifting these barriers has not led to people abusing their medication or returning to drug use (Cunningham et al. 2021; Hageman et al. 2022; Nordeck et al. 2021). Increasing evidence supports the use of low-threshold programs, which do not require drug abstinence for patients beginning treatment (Chalabianloo et al. 2021; Jakubowski and Fox 2020).

Despite clear and consistent research, MAT remains misunderstood by many, who view medication such as buprenorphine as drug use by other means. During the pandemic, the Biden administration refused to extend the

COVID-19 time waiver to expand buprenorphine access without additional restrictions (Diamond 2021) or provide dedicated funding for low-threshold harm reduction treatment. Child welfare staff and judges have shown reluctance to return children to parents successfully stabilized by MAT (Radel et al. 2018). Moreover, successful treatment programs remain few and far between. In the United States, only a third of substance abuse treatment centers even provide MAT (Mojtabai et al. 2019). Significantly, while foster care rates rose in the 2010s, caseloads increased most in counties with the least availability of MAT (Ali and Ghertner 2022).

To truly address the opioid epidemic requires housing and employment services in addition to low-threshold harm reduction treatment programs. Instead, funding goes into the carceral system. Government funds the police force, bankrolls border security, and finances what is perhaps the most potent civil weapon the state has: Child Protective Services. The child welfare system has significant ability to intercede in families—with powers not accorded to any other government institutions except for the criminal justice system. As legal theorist Dorothy Roberts notes, hidden within the child welfare system is a state regime "that sent government agents to invade Black people's homes, kept them under intense and indefinite surveillance, regulated their daily lives, and forcibly separated their families, often permanently" (Roberts 2021).

The Child Welfare System and the Opioid Epidemic

The opioid epidemic has resulted in a dramatic increase in government funding for Child Protective Services, as well as an increase in the number of children entering foster care (Congressional Budget Office 2022; Radel et al. 2018). After a period of decline between 2007 and 2012, the number of children entering foster care began rising steadily (PCSAO 2017; Waite et al. 2018). While changes in child welfare caseloads vary by state, the nationwide increase correlates with overdose deaths and drug-related hospitalizations, both of which are associated with the opioid epidemic (Radel et al. 2018). For every 10 percent increase in hospitalizations due to substance abuse in a single county, the rates of entry into foster care rise by 2 percent (Radel et al. 2018). Even a growth in opioid prescription rates causes an increase in child removals (Quast 2018). The extent of the correlation depends on the state, however, suggesting that the increase is due to local policy more than to an inherent rise in child abuse due to drug use (Freisthler et al. 2022).

Estimates of the percentage of families in the child welfare system with substance abuse issues vary widely, from 8 to 40 percent (Freisthler et al. 2022; Young et al. 2007); exact numbers are difficult to calculate due to varying regional standards for data collection (Seay 2015). An estimated 80 percent or more of all Child Protective Services cases involve allegations of drug use at some point (Sangoi 2020). African American families are disproportionately likely to be identified as having substance abuse issues (Vanderploeg et al. 2007). Moreover, a caseworker's belief that there is substance abuse in the family can outweigh all other risk factors, resulting in higher harm assessments and an increased probability of removal regardless of whether other risk factors are present (Berger et al. 2010; Radel et al. 2018). Court investigators are substantially more likely to rate parents with a history of substance abuse as posing "high risk" to their children, precipitating removal (Young et al. 2007, 141). Children removed because of substance abuse in the family ultimately spend more time in foster care and are more likely to be adopted out than other children (Vanderploeg et al. 2007). Over a third of child removals are attributed to substance misuse by a parent (Children's Bureau 2022; Radel et al. 2018). This percentage has risen sharply over the last two decades: only 10 percent of removals in 2000 were associated with parental substance use, although this number is subject to considerable regional variation (Ghertner et al. 2018). These statistics are generally not broken down by race or income. In the case of prenatal substance exposure, however, racial biases have been well documented. Despite equivalent rates of drug use during pregnancy, Black families are four to ten times more likely to be reported to Child Protective Services (Waite et al. 2018).

The number of children in foster care continues to grow, as CPS separates infants from their drug-involved mothers and the courts impose cruelly long drug sentences, devastating family units. Once in the child welfare system, families have difficulty extracting themselves. Children of mothers with substance abuse issues are removed from home for longer periods, have more negative outcomes in foster care, and are less likely to reunite with their mothers (Moreland et al. 2021).[6] Given the racial biases embedded in the child welfare system, these patterns leave parents rightly concerned: African American mothers have expressed reluctance to seek help for drug addiction because they "fear losing their children to the foster care system if they acknowledge a substance use problem and seek treatment" (Chau 2020, 7). When child welfare policies punish drug addiction, women are less likely to enter treatment (Jessup et al. 2003).

Child abuse is rightly concerning. Abuse of all kinds—spousal, child, elderly—increases in difficult times. During the peak of the COVID-19 pandemic, families faced unprecedented stress, an amalgamation of work losses, childcare dilemmas, and food shortages. Now is a time to be concerned about the most vulnerable among us. The family unit is perhaps more isolated than at any other time in modern history.

At the same time, removing children from the home is its own recipe for disaster. Children are three times more likely to be removed from the home for neglect as opposed to abuse (ACF 2022). There will always be those few yet horrifying cases of abuse where a child clearly cannot remain with their existing guardians. For the majority of cases, however, the statistics are blazingly clear and disturbing. As a group, children removed from their homes have unambiguously worse outcomes: they are less likely to finish high school, let alone go to college; they are more likely to be incarcerated. The problems perpetuate themselves: children placed in foster care are more likely to face removal of their own children (Brännström et al. 2020; Doyle 2013; Rapsey and Rolston 2020). By every measure, children taken by the child welfare system—even if only for a few days—have worse outcomes than those who remain with their families of origin (Sankaran and Church 2017). This includes children of parents undergoing substance use treatment, who do as well staying with their families as they do when they are removed (Hall et al. 2021).

As our nation rethinks entrenched systems of white supremacy and inequality, we should take this moment to similarly question our social programs. Conveniently, many localities have already demonstrated what changes to the foster care system can achieve. Interventions that include family services are less expensive (Johnson-Motoyama et al. 2013) and better at reducing parental substance use and out-of-home placement; they also improve child outcomes and oftentimes increase reunification rates (Kirk and Griffith 2008). Out of billions of dollars of federal funding, however, only a small percentage supports preventive or reunification services; the majority funds foster care and adoption assistance (Congressional Research Service 2022).

Conclusion

The opioid public health crisis began in the 1990s when pharmaceutical companies convinced the medical establishment that opioids were safe for pain management, causing millions of people to become addicted to drugs like OxyContin. The opioid overdose epidemic serves as a lens for viewing how the foster care system operates within the state apparatus. It is easy to scapegoat drug users: former President Trump, for example, expressed early support for President Rodrigo Duterte of the Philippines in his war on drugs. Duterte advocated for the extrajudicial killings of people who are involved with the illegal drug trade, resulting in the deaths of thousands, including at least a hundred children (*Al Jazeera* 2020; Conde 2020). The opioid epidemic similarly played an important rhetorical role in both the 2016 and 2020 presidential elections. Rather than offer compassion, Trump's campaign placed the blame, as usual, on Black and Brown communities (Lingala 2018; Newkirk 2018).

The coronavirus pandemic has reduced life expectancy in the United States by one year—the first time this has occurred since World War II—and by an even more shocking three years for African Americans (Marchione 2021). This historic drop, however, was also driven by the opioid epidemic (Katz and Sanger-Katz 2018; Tanne 2022). Without dramatic changes in our approach to the epidemic and to families, the upward trend will only continue. Moreover, the disparate damage to minority communities causes harms that will reverberate through future generations.

Long after the end of the opioid epidemic, drug use will continue in some form or another (Hawre Jalal et al. 2018). We must be able to address it without causing disproportionate harm to BIPOC communities. The flawed system of Child Protective Services focuses more on punishing parents than on protecting children. The system includes a well-documented legacy of terror. Yet the system continues, targeting families of all identities outside of white cisgendered families. As we write this chapter, there are dozens of bills and several laws encouraging the removal of transgender children from their parents. As long as the foster care system continues, so too will the devastation it leaves in its wake. Racialized capitalism forces our country to create policies that split poor families apart. As the wealth gap widens, the divide between who is and is not potentially subject to the brunt of these cruel policies also widens.

Substance use disorder is a public health crisis and families that are impacted should be treated the same way that we would treat a family impacted by cancer—with love, support, and money. We should invest in families and children, not in family regulation and punishment. We should repeal the Adoption and Safe Families Act of 1997 and instead work to reunite and reestablish families.

Authors' Note

We come to this article from two very different places. One of us has spent decades working with people who use drugs to build political power. The other is a lawyer and legal scholar who has helped keep drug treatment programs open in the wake of community opposition. We have seen the brilliance of people who use drugs, and we know that there is nothing that makes someone who uses drugs less able to raise smart, wonderful, well-adjusted children than anyone else.

Notes

1. According to the CDC (2022), "an estimated 107,622 drug overdose deaths [occurred] in the United States during 2021,"

80,816 of which involved opioids. This number is likely an undercount: researchers estimate that over one-fifth of all opioid deaths go unreported (Boslett et al. 2020).

2. Drug traffickers often exploit women's vulnerability and economic disadvantage to force them into the drug trade (Fleetwood and Leban 2023). Women are also more likely to be used as drug mules, transporting drugs across borders or within countries, thus taking on "the higher-risk, lower-status role" within the drug trade (Harper et al. 2002, 111).

3. For centuries, "[r]acialized definitions of womanhood . . . [have upheld] the rhetoric of white supremacy . . . influenc[ing] a diverse set of legal actions . . . [including] welfare policy, criminal prosecutions, customs, police searches, sexual harassment, and treatment of single mothers" (Walker 2008, 3).

4. Native American children are also significantly overrepresented in the foster care system, representing 2 percent of the foster care population despite being only 1 percent of the general population. In certain states, however, Native American children are overrepresented by a ratio of as much as thirteen to one. At a national level, other minority groups are underrepresented in foster care, albeit with significant state variance (Dettlaff 2020).

5. Adoption and Safe Families Act (ASFA) of 1997, Pub. L. No. 105-89, 111 Stat. 2115 (1997).

6. The mandates of the ASFA, which require that agencies petition to terminate parental rights for children in foster care for fifteen of the past twenty-two months, do not allow for the longer timetables needed for successful recovery from drug addiction (Radel et al. 2018).

References

Administration for Children and Families (ACF). 2022. *Child Maltreatment Report 2020*. Washington, DC: U.S. Department of Health and Human Services.

Alexander, Michelle. 2010. *The New Jim Crow: Mass Incarceration in the Age of Colorblindness*. New York: The New Press.

Alexander, Monica J., Mathew V. Kiang, and Magali Barbieri. 2018. "Trends in Black and White Opioid Mortality in the United States, 1979–2015." *Epidemiology* 29, no. 5 (September): 707–715. https://doi.org/10.1097/EDE.0000000000000858.

Ali, Mir M., and Robin Ghertner. 2022. "Is Buprenorphine Treatment Availability Associated with Decreases in Substantiated Cases of Child Maltreatment?" *Journal of Substance Abuse Treatment* 139 (August): 108780. https://doi.org/10.1016/j.jsat.2022.108780.

Al Jazeera. 2020. "'I Will Kill You': Philippines' Duterte Renews Drug War Threat." June 5, 2020. https://www.aljazeera.com /news/2020/6/5/i-will-kill-you-philippines-duterte-renews-drug -war-threat.

Alpert, Abby, William N. Evans, Ethan M. J. Lieber, and David Powell. 2022. "Origins of the Opioid Crisis and Its Enduring Impacts." *The Quarterly Journal of Economics* 137, no. 2 (May): 1139–1179.

Azagba, Sunday, Lingpeng Shan, Fares Qeadan, and Mark Wolfson. 2021. "Unemployment Rate, Opioids Misuse and Other Substance Abuse: Quasi-Experimental Evidence from Treatment Admissions Data." *BMC Psychiatry* 21, no. 1 (January): 22–29. https://doi.org/10.1186/s12888-020-02981-7.

Bates, Julia. 2016. "The Role of Race in Legitimizing Institutionalization: A Comparative Analysis of Early Child Welfare Initiatives in the United States." *Journal of the History of Childhood & Youth* 9, no. 1 (Winter): 15–28.

Baum, Dan. 2016. "Legalize It All: How to Win the War on Drugs." *Harper's Magazine*, April 2016. https://harpers.org /archive/2016/04/legalize-it-all/.

Beall, Spencer K. 2018. "'Lock Her Up!' How Women Have Become the Fastest-Growing Population in the American Carceral State." *Berkeley Journal of Criminal Law* 23, no. 2 (Spring): 1–39. https://lawcat.berkeley.edu/record/1128438?v=pdf.

Berger, Lawrence M., Kristen S. Slack, Jane Waldfogel, and Sarah K. Bruch. 2010. "Caseworker-Perceived Caregiver Substance Abuse and Child Protective Services Outcomes." *Child Maltreatment* 15, no. 3 (August): 199–210.

Blackmon, Douglas A. 2008. *Slavery by Another Name: The Re-Enslavement of Black Americans from the Civil War to World War II.* New York: Anchor Books.

Boslett, Andrew J., Alina Denham, and Elaine L. Hill. 2020. "Using Contributing Causes of Death Improves Prediction of Opioid Involvement in Unclassified Drug Overdoses in US Death Records." *Addiction* 115, no. 7 (July): 1308–1317.

Brännström, Lars, Bo Vinnerljung, and Anders Hjern. 2020. "Outcomes in Adulthood after Long-Term Foster Care: A Sibling Approach." *Child Maltreatments* 25, no. 4 (November): 383–392.

Brewington, Ericka. 2022. "A Drug Test Is Not a Parenting Test." *Tennesee Tribune,* July 7. https://tntribune.com/a-drug-test-is-not -a-parenting-test/.

Bridges, Khiara M. 2017. *The Poverty of Privacy Rights.* California: Stanford Law Books.

Carson, E. Ann. 2022. *Prisoners in 2021—Statistical Tables.* Washington, DC: Bureau of Justice Statistics. https://bjs.ojp.gov /library/publications/prisoners-2021-statistical-tables.

Center for the Study of Social Policy. 2011. *Disparities and Dispro-portionality in Child Welfare: Analysis of the Research.* Washington, DC. https://assets.aecf.org/m/resourcedoc/AECF-Dispariti esAndDisproportionalityInChildWelfare-2011.pdf.

Centers for Disease Control (CDC). 2022. *U.S. Overdose Deaths in 2021 Increased Half as Much as in 2020—But Are Still Up 15%.* Atlanta, GA. https://www.cdc.gov/nchs/pressroom/nchs_press _releases/2022/202205.htm.

Chalabianloo, Fatemeh, Christian Ohldieck, Øystein Ariansen Haaland, Lars Thore Fadnes, and Kjell Arne Johansson. 2021. "Effectiveness and Safety of Low-Threshold Opioid-Agonist

Treatment in Hard-to-Reach Populations with Opioid Dependence." *European Addiction Research* 28, no. 3 (May): 199–209. https://doi.org/10.1159/000520185.

Chau, Victoria. 2020. "The Opioid Crisis and the Black/African American Population: An Urgent Issue." Publication No. PEP20-05-02-001. Substance Abuse and Mental Health Services Administration.

Children's Bureau. 2022. *The AFCARS Report*. Washington, DC: U.S. Department of Health and Human Services. https://www.acf.hhs.gov/sites/default/files/documents/cb/afcars-report-29.pdf.

Cohen, Aliza, Sheila P. Vakharia, Julie Netherland, and Kassandra Frederique. 2022. "How the War on Drugs Impacts Social Determinants of Health beyond the Criminal Legal System." *Annals of Medicine* 54 (1): 2024–2038.

Conde, Carlos H. 2020. *"Our Happy Family Is Gone": Impact of the "War on Drugs" on Children in the Philippines*. New York: Human Rights Watch. https://www.hrw.org/report/2020/05/27/our-happy-family-gone/impact-war-drugs-children-philippines.

Congressional Budget Office. 2022. *The Opioid Crisis and Recent Federal Policy Responses*. Washington, DC. https://www.cbo.gov/system/files/2022-09/58221-opioid-crisis.pdf.

Congressional Research Service. 2022. *Child Welfare: Purposes, Federal Programs, and Funding*. Washington, DC. https://crsreports.congress.gov/product/pdf/IF/IF10590/31.

Connery, Hilary Smith. 2015. "Medication-Assisted Treatment of Opioid Use Disorder: Review of the Evidence and Future Directions." *Harvard Review of Psychiatry* 23, no. 2 (March–April): 63–75. https://journals.lww.com/hrpjournal/fulltext/2015/03000/medication_assisted_treatment_of_opioid_use.2.aspx.

Courtwright, David T. 2001. *Dark Paradise: A History of Opiate Addiction in America*. Boston, MA: Harvard University Press.

Cunningham, Chinazo O., Laila Khalid, Yuting Deng, Kristine Torres-Lockhart, Mariya Masyukova, Shenell Thomas,

Chenshu Zhang, and Tiffany Lu. 2021. "A Comparison of Office-Based Buprenorphine Treatment Outcomes in Bronx Community Clinics before versus during the COVID-19 Pandemic." *Journal of Substance Abuse Treatment* 135 (April): 108641. https://doi.org/10.1016/j.jsat.2021.108641.

da Costa, Pedro Nicolaci. 2017. "There's a Clear Link between America's Opioid Crisis and Unemployment." *Business Insider*, August 26, 2017. https://www.businessinsider.com/opioid -epidemic-directly-tied-to-higher-unemployment-weak -economy-2017-8.

Dettlaff, Alan J. 2020. "Introduction." In *Racial Disproportionality and Disparities in the Child Welfare System*, edited by Alan J. Dettlaff, 3–8. Cham, Switzerland: Springer Nature.

Dettlaff, Alan J., and Reiko Boyd. 2020. "Racial Disproportionality and Disparities in the Child Welfare System: Why Do They Exist, and What Can Be Done to Address Them?" *The Annals of the American Academy of Political and Social Science* 692, no. 1 (November): 253–274.

Diamond, Dan. 2021. "Biden Kills Buprenorphine Waiver." *Washington Post*, January 27, 2021. https://www.washingtonpost .com/health/2021/01/27/biden-kills-buprenorphine-waiver/.

Doyle, Joseph J. 2013. "Causal Effects of Foster Care: An Instrumental-Variables Approach." *Children & Youth Services Review* 35, no. 7 (July): 1143–1151.

Fairley, Michael, Keith Humphreys, Vilija R. Joyce, Mark Bountha-vong, Jodie Trafton, Ann Combs, Elizabeth M. Oliva, Jeremy D. Goldhaber-Fiebert, Steven M. Asch, Margaret L. Brandeau, and Douglas K. Owens. 2021. "Cost-Effectiveness of Treatments for Opioid Use Disorder." *JAMA Psychiatry* 78, no. 7 (July): 767–777. https://doi.org/10.1001/jamapsychiatry.2021.0247.

Fleetwood, Jennifer, and Lindsay Leban. 2023. "Women's Involve-ment in the Drug Trade: Revisiting the Emancipation Thesis in Global Perspective." *Deviant Behavior* 44 (2): 238–258.

Freisthler, Bridget, Emily Bruce, and Barbara Needell. 2007. "Understanding the Geospatial Relationship of Neighborhood Characteristics and Rates of Maltreatment for Black, Hispanic and White Children." *Social Work* 52, no. 1 (January): 7–16.

Freisthler, Bridget, Nichole Michaels, and Jennifer Price Wolf. 2022. "Families in Crisis: The Relationship between Opioid Overdoses and Child Maltreatment in Neighborhood Areas." *Journal of Studies on Alcohol and Drugs* 83, no. 1 (January): 145–152.

Furr-Holden, Debra, Adam J. Milam, Ling Wang, and Richard Sadler. 2021. "African Americans Now Outpace Whites in Opioid-Involved Overdose Deaths: A Comparison of Temporal Trends from 1999 to 2018." *Addiction* 116, no. 3 (January): 677–683.

Garland, Ann F., Elissa Ellis-MacLeod, John A. Landsverk, William Ganger, and Ivory Johnson. 1998. "Minority Populations in the Child Welfare System: The Visibility Hypothesis Reexamined." *American Journal of Orthopsychiatry* 68 (1): 142–146.

Ghertner, Robin, Annette Waters, Laura Radel, and Gilbert Crouse. 2018. "The Role of Substance Use in Child Welfare Caseloads." *Children and Youth Services Review* 90 (July): 83–93.

Graham, Lorie. 2001. "Reparations and the Indian Child Welfare Act." *Legal Studies Forum* 25: 619–640.

Hageman, Thomas M., Joshua Palmer, Prabir Mullick, and Heeyoung Lee. 2022. "A Buprenorphine Program Evaluation before and during the COVID-19 Pandemic." *The Journal for Nurse Practitioners* 18, no. 3 (March): 267–271. https://doi.org/10.1016/j.nurpra.2021.12.025.

Hager, Thomas. 2019. *Ten Drugs: How Plants, Powders, and Pills Have Shaped the History of Medicine.* New York: Abrams Books.

Hall, Martin T., Aimee B. Kelmel, Ruth A. Huebner, Matthew T. Walton, and Anita P. Barbee. 2021. "Sobriety Treatment and Recovery Teams for Families with Co-Occurring Substance Use and Child Maltreatment: A Randomized Controlled Trial."

Child Abuse & Neglect 114 (April): 104963. https://doi.org/10.1016/j.chiabu.2021.104963.

Haney, Craig, and Philip Zimbardo. 1998. "The Past and Future of U.S. Prison Policy: Twenty-Five Years after the Stanford Prison Experiment." *American Psychologist* 53 (7): 709–727.

Harmon, Mark G., and Breanna Boppre. 2018. "Women of Color and the War on Crime: An Explanation for the Rise in Black Female Imprisonment." *Journal of Ethnicity in Criminal Justice* 16 (4): 309–332.

Harper, Rosalyn L., Gemma C. Harper, and Janet E. Stockdale. 2002. "The Role and Sentencing of Women in Drug Trafficking Crime." *Legal and Criminological Psychology* 7, no. 1 (February): 101–114.

Hedegaard, Holly, Arialdi M. Miniño, and Margaret Warner. 2020. *Drug Overdose Deaths in the United States, 1999–2018.* NCHS Data Brief No. 394. Hyattsville, MD: National Center for Health Statistics.

Hoffman, Kelly M., Sophie Trawalter, Jordan R. Axt, and M. Norman Oliver. 2016. "Racial Bias in Pain Assessment and Treatment Recommendations, and False Beliefs about Biological Differences between Blacks and Whites." *Proceedings of the National Academy of Sciences of the United States of America* 113, no. 16 (April): 4296–4301. https://doi.org/10.1073/pnas.1516047113.

Hughes, Caitlin Elizabeth, and Alex Stevens. 2012. "A Resounding Success or a Disastrous Failure: Re-Examining the Interpretation of Evidence on the Portuguese Decriminalisation of Illicit Drugs." *Drug and Alcohol Review* 31, no. 1 (January): 101–113.

Institute for Clinical and Economic Review (ICER). 2014. *Management of Patients with Opioid Dependence: A Review of Clinical, Delivery System, and Policy Options.* Boston, MA: New England Comparative Effectiveness Public Advisory Council. https://icer.org/wp-content/uploads/2020/10/CEPAC-Opioid-Dependence-Final-Report-For-Posting-July-21.pdf.

Jakubowski, Andrea, and Aaron Fox. 2020. "Defining Low-Threshold Buprenorphine Treatment." *Journal of Addiction Medicine* 14, no. 2 (March/April): 95–98.

Jalal, Hawre, Jeanine M. Buchanich, Mark S. Roberts, Lauren C. Balmert, Kun Zhang, and Donald S. Burke. 2018. "Changing Dynamics of the Drug Overdose Epidemic in the United States from 1979 through 2016." *Science* 361, no. 6408 (September): 1218–1224. https://www.science.org/doi/10.1126/science.aau1184.

Jessup, Martha A., Janice C. Humphreys, and Kathryn A. Lee. 2003. "Extrinsic Barriers to Substance Abuse Treatment among Pregnant Drug Dependent Women." *Journal of Drug Issues* 33 (2): 285–304.

Johnson-Motoyama, Michelle, Jody Brook, Yueqi Yan, and Thomas P. McDonald. 2013. "Cost Analysis of the Strengthening Families Program in Reducing Time to Family Reunification among Substance-Affected Families." *Children and Youth Services Review* 35: 244–252.

Jones, Jonathan S. 2021. "Race and Opioids: Lessons from the Civil War–Era Opioid Addiction Crisis." *Psychiatric Times*, February 25, 2021. https://www.psychiatrictimes.com/view/race-opioids-lessons-civil-war-era-opioid-addiction-crisis.

Kandall, Stephen R. 2010. "Women and Drug Addiction: A Historical Perspective." *Journal of Addictive Diseases* 29, no. 2 (April): 117–126.

Katz, Josh, and Margot Sanger-Katz. 2018. "'The Numbers Are So Staggering.' Overdose Deaths Set a Record Last Year." *New York Times*, November 29, 2018. https://www.nytimes.com/interactive/2018/11/29/upshot/fentanyl-drug-overdose-deaths.html.

Keefe, Patrick Radden. 2017. "The Family That Built an Empire of Pain." *New Yorker*, October 23, 2017. https://www.newyorker.com/magazine/2017/10/30/the-family-that-built-an-empire-of-pain.

Keire, Mara L. 1998."Dope Fiends and Degenerates: The Gendering of Addiction in the Early Twentieth Century." *Journal of Social History* 31, no. 4 (Summer): 809–822.

Kim, Hyunil, Christopher Wildeman, Melissa Jonson-Reid, and Brett Drake. 2017. "Lifetime Prevalence of Investigating Child Maltreatment among US Children." *American Journal of Public Health* 107, no. 2 (February): 274–280.

Kirk, Raymond S., and Diana P. Griffith. 2008. "Impact of Intensive Family Preservation Services on Disproportionality of Out-of-Home Placement of Children of Color in One State's Child Welfare System." *Child Welfare* 87 (5): 87–106.

Kolodny, Andrew, David T. Courtwright, Catherine S. Hwang, Peter Kreiner, John L. Eadie, Thomas W. Clark, and G. Caleb Alexander. 2015. "The Prescription Opioid and Heroin Crisis: A Public Health Approach to an Epidemic of Addiction." *Annual Review of Public Health* 36 (1): 559–574. https://doi.org/10.1146/annurev-publhealth-031914-122957.

Lamonica, Aukje, and Miriam Boeri. 2020. "Stories of Loss: Separation of Children and Mothers Who Use Opioids." *Journal of Ethnographic and Qualitative Research* 15, no. 1 (Fall): 63–81. https://www.ncbi.nlm.nih.gov/pmc/articles/PMC8493853/.

Lenox, Marne L. 2011. "Neutralizing the Gendered Collateral Consequences of the War on Drugs." *NYU Law Review* 86 (1): 280–315. https://www.nyulawreview.org/issues/volume-86-number-1/neutralizing-the-gendered-collateral-consequences-of-the-war-on-drugs/.

Lexchin, Joel, and Jillian Clare Kohler. 2011. "The Danger of Imperfect Regulation: OxyContin Use in the United States and Canada." *The International Journal of Risk & Safety in Medicine* 23 (4): 233–240.

Lingala, Krish. 2018. "Trump's Opioid Plan and the Bones of the War on Drugs." *Pacific Standard*, April 3, 2017. https://psmag.com/news/trumps-opioid-plan-and-the-bones-of-the-war-on-drugs.

Luigi, Mimosa, Michael Luo, and Etienne J. P. Maes. 2021. "Buprenorphine Opioid Treatment during the COVID-19 Pandemic" (Comment). *JAMA Internal Medicine* 181, no. 8 (August): 1135. https://doi.org/10.1001/jamainternmed.2021.0777.

Maguire-Jack, Kathryn, Sarah A. Font, and Rebecca Dillard. 2020. "Child Protective Services Decision-Making: The Role of Children's Race and County Factors." *American Journal of Orthopsychiatry* 90 (1): 48–62.

Marchione, Marilynn. 2021. "US Life Expectancy Drops a Year in Pandemic, Most Since WWII." *Associated Press*, February 17, 2021. https://apnews.com/article/us-life-expectancy-huge -decline-f4caaf4555563d09e927f1798136a869.

Matthews, Timothy A., Grace Sembajwe, Roland von Känel, and Jian Li. 2022. "Associations of Employment Status with Opioid Misuse: Evidence from a Nationally Representative Survey in the U.S." *Journal of Psychiatric Research* 151 (July): 30–33.

Mazure, Carolyn M., and David A. Fiellin. 2018. "Women and Opioids: Something Different Is Happening Here." *The Lancet* 392, no. 10141 (July): 9–11.

Milaney, Katrina, Jenna Passi, Lisa Zaretsky, Tong Liu, Claire M. O'Gorman, Leslie Hill, and Daniel Dutton. 2021. "Drug Use, Homelessness and Health: Responding to the Opioid Overdose Crisis with Housing and Harm Reduction Services." *Harm Reduction Journal* 18, article no. 92. https://harmreductionjournal .biomedcentral.com/articles/10.1186/s12954-021-00539-8.

Mojtabai, Ramin, Christine Mauro, Melanie M. Wall, Colleen L. Barry, and Mark Olfson. 2019. "Medication Treatment for Opioid Use Disorders in Substance Use Treatment Facilities." *Health Affairs* 38, no. 1 (January): 14–23. https://www .healthaffairs.org/doi/10.1377/hlthaff.2018.05162.

Morden, Nancy E., Deanna Chyn, Andrew Wood, and Ellen Meara. 2021. "Racial Inequality in Prescription Opioid Receipt—Role of Individual Health Systems." *The New England Journal of Medicine* 385, no. 4 (July): 342–351. https://www.nejm .org/doi/10.1056/NEJMsa2034159.

Moreland, Angela, Carla Newman, Kat Crum, and Funlola Area. 2021. "Types of Child Maltreatment and Child Welfare Involvement among Opioid-Using Mothers Involved in

Substance Use Treatment." *Children and Youth Services Review* 126 (July): 106021. https://doi.org/10.1016/j.childyouth.2021 .106021.

National Bureau of Economic Research (NBER). 2017. "Are Opioid Deaths Affected by Macroeconomic Conditions?" *Bulletin on Aging & Health*, August 15, 2017. https://www.nber.org/bah /2017n03/are-opioid-deaths-affected-macroeconomic -conditions.

National Council of Juvenile and Family Court Judges (NJCFCJ). 2017 *Technical Assistance Bulletin: Disproportionality Rates for Children of Color in Foster Care (Fiscal Year 2015)*. Reno, NV: National Council of Juvenile and Family Court Judges.

National Institute on Drug Abuse (NIDA). 2021. "ADAPT-2 Trial Results Deliver a Breakthrough in Long Search for Methamphet-amine Use Disorder Medication." https://archives.nida.nih.gov /news-events/noras-blog/2021/01/adapt-2-trial-results-deliver -breakthrough-in-long-search-methamphetamine-use-disorder -medication.

Netherland, Julie, and Helena Hansen. 2016. "The War on Drugs That Wasn't: Wasted Whiteness, 'Dirty Doctors,' and Race in Media Coverage of Prescription Opioid Misuse." *Culture, Medicine and Psychiatry* 40, no. 4 (June): 664–686.

———. 2017. "White Opioids: Pharmaceutical Race and the War on Drugs That Wasn't." *Biosocieties* 12, no. 2 (June): 217–238.

Newkirk, Vann R. 2018. "The People Trump's War on Drugs Will Actually Punish." *The Atlantic*, March 26, 2018. https://www .theatlantic.com/politics/archive/2018/03/killing-drug-dealers -opioid-epidemic/555782/.

Noah, Lars. 2019. "Federal Regulatory Responses to the Prescription Opioid Crisis: Too Little, Too Late?" *Utah Law Review* 4 (1): 757–784.

Nordeck, Courtney D., Megan Buresh, Noa Krawczyk, Michael Fingerhood, and Deborah Agus. 2021. "Adapting a Low-Threshold Buprenorphine Program for Vulnerable Populations during the COVID-19 Pandemic." *Journal of Addiction Medicine* 15, no. 5 (September–October): 364–369.

Nunes, Edward V., Frances R. Levin, Muredach P. Reilly, and Nabila El-Bassel. 2021. "Medication Treatment for Opioid Use Disorder in the Age of COVID-19: Can New Regulations Modify the Opioid Cascade?" *Journal of Substance Abuse Treatment* 122 (March): 108196. https://doi.org/10.1016/j.jsat.2020.108196.

Om, Anjali. 2018. "The Opioid Crisis in Black and White: The Role of Race in Our Nation's Recent Drug Epidemic." *Journal of Public Health* 40, no. 4 (December): 614–615. https://doi.org/10.1093/pubmed/fdy103.

Provance, Jim. 2022. "Women More Likely in Prison Due to Drugs Than Men, Study Finds." *The Blade* (Toledo, OH), June 15, 2022. https://www.toledoblade.com/local/courts/2022/06/15/women-more-likely-in-prison-due-to-drugs-than-men-study-finds/stories/20220615110.

Public Children Services Association of Ohio (PCSAO). 2017. *The Opioid Epidemic's Impact on Children Services in Ohio*. http://www.pcsao.org/pdf/advocacy/OpioidBriefingSlidesUpdated12-17.pdf.

Puzzanchera, Charles, and Moriah Taylor. 2020. *Disproportionality Rates for Children of Color in Foster Care Dashboard*. Reno, NV: National Council of Juvenile and Family Court Judges.

Quast, Troy, Eric A. Storch, and Svetlana Yampolskaya. 2018. "Opioid Prescription Rates and Child Removals: Evidence from Florida." *Health Affairs* 37, no. 1 (January): 134–139. https://doi.org/10.1377/hlthaff.2017.1023.

Radel, Laura, Melinda Baldwin, Gilbert Crouse, Robin Ghertner, and Annette Waters. 2018. *Substance Use, the Opioid Epidemic, and the Child Welfare System: Key Findings from a Mixed Methods Study*. Washington, DC: U.S. Department of Health and Human Services.

Raikhel, Eugene, and William Garriott. 2013. *Addiction Trajectories*. Durham, NC: Duke University Press.

Rapsey, Charlene, and Cassandra J. Rolston. 2020. "Fostering the Family, Not Just the Child: Exploring the Value of a Residential Family Preservation Programme from the Perspectives of Service Users and Staff." *Children & Youth Services Review* 108, no. 8 (November): 104505–104535.

Ritchie, Andrea. 2017. *Invisible No More: Police Violence against Black Women and Women of Color*. Boston, MA: Beacon Press.

Roberts, Dorothy. 2002. *Shattered Bonds: The Color of Child Welfare*. New York: Civitas Books.

———. 2021. "Abolish Family Policing, Too: The Child Welfare System Is a Powerful State Policing Apparatus That Functions to Regulate Poor and Working-Class Families." *Dissent*, Summer 2021. https://www.dissentmagazine.org/article/abolish -family-policing-too/.

———. 2022. *Torn Apart: How the Child Welfare System Destroys Black Families—and How Abolition Can Build a Safer World*. New York: Basic Books.

Samuels, Elizabeth A., Seth A. Clark, Caroline Wunsch, Lee Ann Jordison Keeler, Neha Reddy, Rahul Vanjani, and Rachel S. Wightman. 2020. "Innovation during COVID-19: Improving Addiction Treatment Access." *Journal of Addiction Medicine* 14, no. 4 (July/August): 8–9.

Sangoi, Lisa. 2020. *"Whatever They Do, I'm Her Comfort, I'm Her Protector": How the Foster System Has Become Ground Zero for the U.S. Drug War*. New York: Movement for Family Power.

Sankaran, Vivek S., and Christopher Church. 2017. "Easy Come, Easy Go: The Plight of Children Who Spend Less Than Thirty Days in Foster Care." *University of Pennsylvania Journal of Law and Social Change* 19 (3): 207–237.

Seay, Kristen. 2015. "How Many Families in Child Welfare Services Are Affected by Parental Substance Use Disorders? A Common Question That Remains Unanswered." *Child Welfare* 94 (4): 19–51. https://www.ncbi.nlm.nih.gov/pmc/articles /PMC4894838/.

Serdarevic, Mirsada, Catherine W. Striley, and Linda B. Cottler. 2017. "Gender Differences in Prescription Opioid Use." *Current Opinion in Psychiatry* 30, no. 4 (July): 238–246.

Stephens, Tricia, Alexis Kuerbis, Caterina Pisciotta, and Jon Morgenstern. 2020. "Underexamined Points of Vulnerability for Black Mothers in the Child Welfare System: The Role of Number of Births, Age of First Use of Substances and Criminal Justice Involvement." *Children and Youth Services Review* 108 (January): 104557.

Tanne, Janice Hopkins. 2022. "US Life Expectancy Reaches 25 Year Low." *BMJ (Online)* 379 (December): o3063.

Terplan, Mishka. 2017. "Women and the Opioid Crisis: Historical Context and Public Health Solutions." *Fertility and Sterility* 108, no. 2 (August): 195–199. https://www.fertstert.org/article/S0015-0282(17)30431-4/fulltext.

Trickey, Erick. 2018. "Inside the Story of America's 19th-Century Opiate Addiction." *Smithsonian Magazine*, January 4, 2018. https://www.smithsonianmag.com/history/inside-story-americas-19th-century-opiate-addiction-180967673.

Trivedi, Shanta. 2022. "The Adoption and Safe Families Act Is Not Worth Saving: The Case for Repeal." *Family Court Review* (forthcoming 2023). http://dx.doi.org/10.2139/ssrn.4201525.

Vanderploeg, Jeffrey J., Christian M. Connell, Colleen Caron, Leon Saunders, Karol H. Katz, and Jacob Kraemer Tebes. 2007. "The Impact of Parental Alcohol or Drug Removals on Foster Care Placement Experiences: A Matched Comparison Group Study." *Child Maltreatment* 12, no. 2 (May): 125–136.

Van Zee, Art. 2009. "The Promotion and Marketing of Oxycontin: Commercial Triumph, Public Health Tragedy." *American Journal of Public Health* 99, no. 2 (February): 221–227. https://doi.org/10.2105/AJPH.2007.131714.

Vitale, Alex. 2018. *The End of Policing*. New York: Verso.

Waite, Douglas, Mary V. Greiner, and Zach Laris. 2018. "Putting Families First: How the Opioid Epidemic Is Affecting Children and Families, and the Child Welfare Policy Options to Address It." *Journal of Applied Research on Children* 9 (1): 1–35. https:// digitalcommons.library.tmc.edu/childrenatrisk/vol9/iss1/4/.

Wakeman, Sarah E. 2016. "Using Science to Battle Stigma in Addressing the Opioid Epidemic: Opioid Agonist Therapy Saves Lives." *American Journal of Medicine* 129, no. 5 (May): 455–456. https://doi.org/10.1016/j.amjmed.2015.12.028.

Walker, Bela August. 2008. "Fractured Bonds: Policing Whiteness & Womanhood through Race-Based Marriage Annulments." *DePaul Law Review* 58 (1): 1–50.

Wang, Linda, Jeffrey Weiss, Elizabeth Bogel Ryan, Justine Waldman, Stacey Rubin, and Judy L. Griffin. 2021. "Telemedicine Increases Access to Buprenorphine Initiation during the COVID-19 Pandemic." *Journal of Substance Abuse Treatment* 124 (May): 108272. https://www.jsatjournal.com/article/S0740 -5472(20)30529-8/fulltext.

Wiercigroch, David, Hasan Sheikh, and Jennifer Hulme. 2020. "A Rapid Access to Addiction Medicine Clinic Facilitates Treatment of Substance Use Disorder and Reduces Substance Use." *Substance Abuse Treatment, Prevention, and Policy* 15, no. 4 (January): 1–10. https://doi.org/10.1186/s13011-019-0250-1.

Wildeman, Christopher, and Natalia Emanuel. 2014. "Cumulative Risks of Foster Care Placement by Age 18 for U.S. Children, 2000–2011." *PloS One* 9, no. 3 (March): e92785. https://doi.org/10 .1371/journal/pone.0092785.

Wilson, Nana, Jeffrey Weiss, Elizabeth Bogel Ryan, Justine Waldman, Stacey Rubin, and Judy L. Griffin. 2020. "Drug and Opioid-Involved Overdose Deaths—United States, 2017–2018." *Morbidity & Mortality Weekly Report* 69: 290–297. https://www .cdc.gov/mmwr/volumes/69/wr/mm6911a4.htm.

Yamamoto, Ayae, Jack Needleman, Lillian Gelberg, Gerald Kominski, Steven Shoptaw, and Yusuke Tsugawa. 2019. "Association between Homelessness and Opioid Overdose and

Opioid-Related Hospital Admissions/Emergency Department Visits." *Social Science & Medicine* 242 (December): 112585–112596.

Young, Nancy K., Sharon M. Boles, and Cathleen Otero. 2007. "Parental Substance Use Disorders and Child Maltreatment: Overlap, Gaps, and Opportunities." *Child Maltreatment* 12, no. 2 (May): 137–149.

4

Memories of Two Pandemics

MARCIA M. GALLO AND CARMEN VÁZQUEZ

Marcie, April 12, 2021

What feels like eons ago now—March 8, 2020—my spouse Ann Cammett and I organized a small dinner party at our home in Manhattan. Little did we know then that it would be the last social gathering we would host for well over a year. We knew that life as we had been living it was changing. We just didn't know how much.

That night, the alarming spread of the new variant of the coronavirus—COVID-19—was a big topic of conversation. New York's Governor Andrew Cuomo had declared a state of emergency the day before, on March 7, 2020, when the state reported seventy-six cases. Those of us gathered around the dining room table—a group that included two gay men (Martin Duberman and Eli Zal) and two other lesbians (Terry Boggis and Carmen Vázquez)—had been active in the LGBTQ+ movements in New York and San Francisco since at least the 1980s. It was not surprising that we who had lived through the onset of the HIV/AIDS epidemic drew comparisons between then and now, especially as the realities of the new virus and its impact were starting to alter everything.

The statistics in those early days were frightening. By March 15, there were 729 COVID-19 cases in New York—a big increase in just one week—with 3 deaths; the next day, schools were closed statewide as were movie theaters, gyms, and casinos; restaurants and bars were limited to take-out and delivery services. Anyone who was deemed "nonessential" was ordered to begin working from home. Five days later, on March 20, there were 7,102 reported cases and 46 deaths. That day, the governor officially put New York State "on pause" and shut down all non-essential businesses. Six-foot social distancing requirements were implemented in all public settings; people 70 years of age or older were ordered to stay home.

In what felt like a sudden onslaught, our vibrant lives changed radically. During those first weeks and months of the COVID-19 pandemic, some people who had personal and political experiences of the early years of HIV/AIDS were thinking and writing about both pandemics. In mid-March, my friend Elaine Elinson sent me Kevin Fong's (2020) piece in *Yes!* Magazine about coming out in San Francisco in the early AIDS years. At about the same time, radio host Laura Flanders interviewed former Queers for Economic Justice director Kenyon Farrow on "Inequality and COVID 19" (Farrow 2020). The *Boston Review* published Michael Bronski's article on AIDS and the coronavirus in April 2020 and Sarah Schulman put the finishing touches on her expansive history of ACT UP New York, *Let the Record Show*, which was published in May 2021. Kraig Pannell, who had worked with Carmen at the New York State Department of Health, was in the thick of advocating for LGBTQ+ people and thus dealing with both pandemics on a daily basis.

As Mathew Rodriguez (2020) wrote for *The Body* in April,

these viruses are different scientifically: HIV and COVID-19 have little in common as to how they are transmitted and how they affect the human body on the inside. But, in the way that they affect the body politic, the citizenry, they have dusted up many of society's worst impulses: the need to blame, to criminalize, to lock each other up. And it is in these comparisons where we can look to what we know from the AIDS epidemic as guidance.

The initial wave of infection and deaths from COVID-19 revealed the racial, gendered, and sexual fissures in American society. Like those who died during the first decade of the HIV/AIDS crisis, the first to succumb to COVID-19 experienced social injustices and stigma. Queer people, Haitians, and drug users were the villains then; today members of the Asian American and Pacific Islander communities face brutal assaults.

A hallmark of both pandemics was the intervention (or lack thereof) of the federal government, which reinforced unequal access to health care and other essential services. In the first half-dozen years of HIV/AIDS as well as at the onset of COVID-19 in 2020, the federal response was absent, inaccurate, ineffective. Our so-called leaders would not address or admit the seriousness of the virus, fueling misinformation and panic. The malfeasance of the Reagan and Trump administrations exacerbated the impact of both pandemics and their rapid, deadly spreads.

One of the biggest challenges in 2020 was that COVID-19 enforced "social distancing" as a crucial way to prevent the spread of the virus. For those of us who lived in one of the AIDS "hot spots" in the early years of the crisis, the fear of physical contact during the COVID pandemic was reminiscent of the initial misinformation and confusion about how HIV was transmitted. Too many people literally lost touch with their friends and loved ones until public health authorities established that HIV was spread via the exchange of bodily fluids. We were then able to come together, coalesce, and create care communities, large and small—friendship circles, health and welfare teams, activist groups. We shared the pain and fear with our loved ones, in person and up close. In 2020, scientists rapidly discovered that COVID-19 is an airborne virus. The physical separation that was needed to prevent infection during the pandemic's first year meant isolation from family, friends, and necessary communities of care and support. While the new virus and its rapid spread have had devastating consequences, the development and increasing availability of vaccines in the United States over the last few months (which do not yet exist for HIV) provide relief and hope for some semblance of normalcy.

But it was because of the imperative to stay home and stay apart that Carmen and I agreed to share our San Francisco memories in writing with each another. As lovers and partners from 1984 to 1996, we had lived and worked as organizers in San Francisco during the discovery, disarray, and devastation of AIDS. In 2020, after more than thirty-five years of friendship, and despite some "dyke drama," we saw ourselves as family. After discussing the idea briefly at the March 8 dinner party, we began to email back and forth, adding our thoughts whenever one of us recorded another memory of the people, places, and political events from the 1980s and 1990s generated by our current situations. It was not a dialogue but a free-form diary of our pasts and presents.

The history we shared very much informed our current perspectives, as did the seemingly magical place we had called home for nearly twenty-five years. The personal and political possibilities in San Francisco had seemed endless to both of us. As Carmen remembered in June 2020,

> [b]etween 1971 and 1981, when the full horror of AIDS began unveiling itself, there was a frenzy of social and political activism and community organizing that laid the foundation for what would become the fight back against AIDS by San Francisco's Queer activists. . . . We were celebrating, moving the forces of Justice and Liberation forward. . . . We could not yet see the dark storms heading our way, the political storms, the viral storm and how they would come together to kill thousands of us.

For so many of us, San Francisco had been a beacon of positive change.

In composing our shared memories, we lifted up some of the people, both celebrated and lesser known, who had touched our lives, such as lesbian and gay leaders Pat Norman, Phyllis Lyon, and Del Martin; Richard Sevilla, Doug Warner, and Reggie Williams; and many more. All of them were part of vibrant and resilient LGBTQ+ and progressive communities with local, national, and international influence. As activists, Carmen and I also valued groups ranging from the ACLU to the Alliance Against Women's Oppression, from the National Task Force on AIDS to the Sisters of Perpetual Indulgence, and we incorporated the sisters and brothers of our families of birth into our extended personal and political networks. But we also shared the horror of public catastrophes as well as the heartbreak of private losses, from the 1978 murders of Mayor George Moscone and Supervisor Harvey Milk to the devastation of our communities due to HIV/AIDS, events that were less than five years apart.

The memories that Carmen and I documented in 2020 resulted in a sometimes surprising, always very personal account of two devastatingly cruel crises that, in Rodriguez's words, "dusted up many of society's worst impulses." While we do not yet know the final death toll of either HIV/AIDS or COVID-19, we do know that both of them have taken too many loved ones from us.

Carmen, March 22, 2020

I sit at my computer at a place called the Larches in Woods Hole, Massachusetts, on Cape Cod. I stare out the window at sun-dappled larches and evergreens swaying toward the sun.

It is my coronavirus place of quarantine. I worry myself sick over my family and friends in my beloved New York City and Texas. I rage at the ineptness and hubris of the President of the United States.

And I remember.

Panicked citizens wore masks and first responders wore gloves. Some didn't even respond to the crisis.

Their government did nothing until thousands had died.

Ultimately, more than 700,000 died.

It was 1982 in San Francisco and New York, not 2020. It wasn't the coronavirus. It was AIDS.

SAN FRANCISCO, 1982

Memories rush in unbridled. Steve and his sandy shock of hair. Muscles ripped. In love with laughing. We went to LA for a conference and skipped off to Disneyland because we were young and queer. And why not? I hated roller coasters as a child and even more as an adult. Steve laughed my fears away. He promised to protect me. I screamed the entire ride and dug into those beefy arms, clinging to sanity but barely.

When we dismounted, I saw blue and purple bruises everywhere my hands and fingers had dug into him. He laughed. Called me strong dyke! We went for martinis.

Steve died at San Francisco General Hospital three weeks later.

Castro Street was a buzzing, vibrant, very crowded street when I arrived in San Francisco in 1974. They said of the city that the men were beautiful and the women were strong. Lovers kissing and holding hands in broad daylight! I was mesmerized and innocent, less than a decade away from the epidemic that would turn Castro's glitter into the haunting grey of young men struggling to walk and breathe.

I remember Pat Norman. Tall, gorgeous woman. Black and Native American features blended to create an Amazon. She had been my counselor for a year and now served as the San Francisco Health Department coordinator of Lesbian and Gay Health Services. I was beginning my tenure at the Women's Building with all its attendant turmoil. Race and class fissures between the white women and the women of color. The lesbian feminist separatists and the rest of us. The policewomen who wanted to call it home and the immigrant women who wanted no San Francisco Police Department signs on the meeting board. Del Martin and Phyllis Lyon, aghast that we would turn down the policewomen. There were bombings and bomb threats, and a fire.

The first cases of what would later become known as AIDS were reported in the United States in June 1981. Pat Norman was a calm, rational woman, not one given to hyperbole or sensation. By early 1982, when she made her rounds to the health centers, bathhouses, bars, and other community gathering sites to talk about gay-related immune deficiency (GRID), or the "gay cancer," few believed her.

It was ridiculous. You can't get a cancer because you're gay! It's a government plot to shut down the bathhouses and run us back into closets! Spread by sex? No way, no way, no way.

We weren't giving up our freedom, our bathhouses, and never our sex! We didn't know about the people in Africa or the hemophiliacs or the drug users. We didn't know then, but we would, eventually.

By the end of 1981, there were 270 reported cases of severe immune deficiency among gay men—121 men had died.

MARCH 23, 2020

A deer and her fawns came to visit today. They stood and watched the cars in the driveway, curious but unafraid. There is no hunting on the Larches.

I looked in the *New York Times* at pictures of streets empty of humans. Las Ramblas in Spain. Place de la Concorde in Paris. A lone diner in Beijing. An empty beach in Los Angeles. Boats without passengers in Srinagar, India. A green lamp shining on an empty street in Bangkok. The Earth is closed.

SAN FRANCISCO, 1989

I remember Richard Sevilla. Plucked from the novellas my mother watched. Tall, handsome, winsome in his lawyer suits, cow-brown eyes shining with love for his people and his work at La Raza Centro Legal. He and I stopped counting the funeral services after fifty. They blurred in rituals of tears and farewells and anger. The newly formed San Francisco AIDS Office and San Francisco AIDS Foundation were formed by and for white gay men. Brown and Black men, many closeted from their families and isolated from a gay community scene that was disappearing by the day, were not prevention targets. The Gay Latino Alliance (GALA) was dying. Esta Noche, the Latino gay bar founded by GALA, was a magnet for HIV. Richard was heartbroken.

Richard was responsible for my award from La Raza Centro Legal in 1989. I brought my mother—"Mamacita"—in from NYC for the gala and basked in the resplendence of her pride. Richard preened. A fine lady in a crimson dress asked if I was a waiter. *No, ma'am. I am the awardee.* I loved Richard for the gift of that night.

Today, I search for his name for an hour and three meager references come up. Three lines. No picture.

My turn for heartbreak, Richard.

I think of our outrage at the weeks that went by without word from our government about the threat of the coronavirus and the bungled rollout of testing we have endured. I remember the four years it took for the Reagan administration to begin funding AIDS prevention and treatment after thousands had died.

I think of the sex workers who died then and will die now because they're not getting any checks from the government and their customers aren't coming back. How many of them will be joining the ranks of the homeless and the most at risk? Like their gay brothers before them thirty-eight years ago, they will be denied compassion, resources, hope, and their lives.

Maybe in an alternate universe, HIV would be exclusively transmitted through heterosexual contact, leaving the queers to inherit the Earth. What would *that* pandemic have looked like?

What would we have done?

Marcie, March 25, 2020

SAN FRANCISCO, 1980S

Doug Warner was bright and beautiful, energetic (sometimes frenetic), small and sturdy with an outsized personality. Blazing-blue eyes, quick wit, keen intelligence. Sophisticated and well-educated, raised in a rural white working-class family on Long Island, the one of his generation who "got out." Left Yale early, moved to San Francisco. Became a lawyer. We met when I "hired" him at the local ACLU office as an intake counselor, a volunteer position. He soon became a force to be reckoned with.

He was my best friend, co-worker, comrade, and co-conspirator, my angel and my devil. I loved him dearly, cherished his attention, craved his brilliance, coped with his outrageousness, quarreled with him over his purposefully politically incorrect attitudes and comments. He told me what to plant in my gardens. I followed him to wild all-night dancing orgies at The Stud, drank his champagne, and snorted his coke.

We were lovers, briefly, until he reminded me that he was, after all, a gay man. More than thirty years later, I still have the card he sent me during our "breakup"; it featured an R. L. Stine–like drawing of a woman digging a grave, head-lined "Woman Trying Frantically to Bury Deep Feelings."

And I did try. I tried to stop desiring him. I tried—and succeeded—in putting a different face on our unbalanced romance, to revise the intensity of our commitment, to step back and see what <u>was</u> instead of what I wanted it to be.

It wasn't until well after a long-desired trip to Italy in 1989 that I realized I had encountered a technique used by artists throughout the centuries. On this trip that led me from the lake region of northern Italy to the island of Capri, I became fascinated by *trompe l'oeil*, the device of "fooling the eye" to see density, and intricate detail, on a flat surface. It was every-where—in church frescoes, streets, and alleyways—and was featured in many famous paintings displayed in museums great and small from Rapallo to Firenze. Looking back now, I understand that Doug's multilayered, careful presentations of himself as healthy and always in control, especially in the early years of the AIDS epidemic, effectively fooled many of us. Especially me.

He was a leader in the gay rights movement in San Francisco in the 1980s, working closely with the ACLU as well as Bay Area Lawyers for Individual Freedom, where he provided counseling for callers to the AIDS Legal Referral Panel. Doug put his considerable personal and professional energies to work on expanding and ensuring basic civil liberties before and during the outbreak of the virus. He died at age thirty-eight, one of the hundreds of thousands of people that it claimed.

By then I shared him with a circle of friends in a "family we chose," as Kath Weston (1997) described it. In the tumultuous years before gay marriage was even remotely on the LGBTQ+ horizon, when we fought for basic rights to live, love, teach, and form communities, our chosen family included lesbians, gay men, bi and straight coworkers and colleagues, kids and elders. Doug was at the center of it all.

Memories of Doug and his ability to "fool the eye" suddenly rushed back to me during the first weeks and months of the COVID-19 pandemic, when I saw an Italian newspaper filled with tiny photographs and brief biographies of the people who had succumbed to this bizarre new plague.

Instantly, I was transported back decades to the days, weeks, months of obituary pages just like this one, especially in one of San Francisco's most popular gay newspapers, the *Bay Area Reporter*, which chronicled the rapidly increasing number of deaths to HIV/AIDS. But in the 1980s and early '90s, the photos were mostly of young, often beautiful, white men with a smattering of Black and Latino and Asian faces among them. Very few women. Why were there so few?

Then, the weekly newsprint HIV/AIDS memorials to friends, acquaintances, strangers, local celebrities, and family members were potent visual reminders of the vibrant lives lost to a strange new disease. Then, as now, our federal government deemed those we lost as insignificant, if not deserving, of such awful deaths, snickering and snidely giving credence to the horrible homophobic sentiment that "maybe they deserved it." It took handsome leading-man celebrity Rock Hudson's sickness and death—he was a close friend of the Reagan family—to shut some of them up. But they still failed to act.

In many ways it was the death of a dream. San Francisco in the 1980s and '90s had provided a perfect place to create our own particular "Tales of the City." It was a magical queer country, a shining example of new possibilities, but starting in the summer of 1981 it began to morph—slowly at first, then rapidly—into a disastrous no-man's-land, with its terrible mix of love and intimacy, sickness and sudden deaths, bogus funerals and heartfelt memorial services.

It wasn't until I returned from Firenze in late October 1989—having cut short my trip in reaction to Carmen's panic over the physical and personal traumas unleashed in the Bay Area by the Loma Prieta earthquake—that I first learned that Doug was HIV positive. He was starting to exhibit symptoms that could not be ignored.

We were crouched down together in my garden on a bright blue late fall day, examining the geraniums and calla lilies as we debated what to plant for spring, when I saw the purplish bruise on his leg. I knew what it meant. He knew I knew what it meant. With my heart in my throat, I asked him about it. He tried to reassure me, to play it off as no big deal, to remind me that he was in local clinical trials due to a history of STDs, getting the best care possible. He would be fine. It was going to be okay.

Less than four months later, on Valentine's Day, he was gone.

Carmen, March 26, 2020

Day 9 of our quarantine.

My refuge is a place called The Little House. She is a shingled, weather-beaten, brown-turned-grey old New England beauty built in 1926. She shelters us from the cold, racoons, wild turkeys, skunks, foxes, coyotes, and other inhabitants of the Larches. There's not much walking after dark.

Yesterday, the alleged President of the United States opined that perhaps we have overreacted. We need to get back to work and open up for business, despite the protestations of public health officials. Flu and cars kill people too. Idiot.

Open it back up, even if millions get infected and thousands die. God forbid the stock market should continue to fall. The man has his priorities.

SAN FRANCISCO, 1987

I remember Rocco. Beautiful Rocco with the jet-black hair and drooping eyelids, languid and sexy even when he was perfectly still. He was Douglas Warner's lover—another lost to AIDS. Rocco sang Cole Porter songs in small piano bars, in any bar. He made us all swoon.

I would close my eyes and see Cole Porter, his hands stroking the piano keys, pouring out all those songs of love and wit and longing. Married with many a homosexual affair, a queer with a wife. He composed and sang when those like him were considered sick. Fifty years after the riding accident that crippled Cole Porter, his young emulator channeled him and maybe his sadness. Rocco didn't have a wife. He had a queer lover who was to die soon. Maybe Rocco knew.

In The Little House in 2020, I watch the turkeys and the deer. Carlie is home-schooling the kids. Erica is working long distance and sometimes having virtual happy hours with her co-workers. I play solitaire and read a mystery, tend the fire, take my turn at making dinner or cleaning. A commune by any other name. For the moment, I feel protected from the fucking invisible virus enemy. But for how long? I am scared. I am scared for my family and for myself. I try to imagine the future, but when I close my eyes it's just a blank white canvass. I haven't felt this way since AIDS.

I have a fantasy of all sex workers and all the homeless and all the people living with HIV and all their families and friends linking arms around the White House wearing masks and gloves and red coronavirus hats and shouting *Shame to the naked emperor! Shame! Shame! Shame!* Shame.

And I remember what social solidarity looked like at the height of the AIDS pandemic.

Marcie, March 27, 2020

We are now officially "on pause," according to the Governor of New York. What does that mean for the folks who can't "pause"? Those considered "essential workers" fit into an extremely broad category—with women over-represented. Will we see the same silence regarding gender disparities now as we did during the AIDS crisis?

As activist historian Jennifer Brier reminded us in her *Washington Post* opinion piece published in March 2020, "We can't forget women as we tell the story of COVID-19." She wrote, "Despite women's long-standing work, white gay men dominate our historical memory of HIV/AIDS. . . . But Black women and Latinas (and women who are Afro-Latina and/or of Caribbean origins) have also been part of this history since the official start of the epidemic in 1981. They were among the first people infected with HIV and to die from AIDS." Significantly, HIV-positive women also led the fight against AIDS by organizing to expand the definition of who had the disease. As of 1990, the only way a person could move from being classified as HIV positive to being diagnosed with AIDS was to develop a set of conditions that appeared in men's bodies as their immune systems deteriorated from the virus. This had major ramifications for health care as women were frequently denied coverage because the ways their immune systems manifested the disease did not align with what men experienced. So women mobilized to fight for change. At protests in Washington, DC, women living with HIV/AIDS carried signs that read: "Women Don't Get AIDS, They Just Die From It" (Brier 2020). Today, the realities for women facing COVID-19 are stark due to long-standing gender inequalities. As noted in a United Nations policy brief on the impact of COVID-19 on women, "even the limited gains made in the past decades are at risk of being rolled back. . . . Across every sphere, from health to the economy, security to social protection, the impacts of COVID-19 are exacerbated for women and girls simply by virtue of their sex" (United Nations 2020, 2).

Carmen, March 28, 2020

I sit on the back porch soaking in some sun on the first day that feels like spring since I got here. I see ghosts of AIDS past and COVID-19 present. I think of the men and women caring for the sick all over the world. Today they know the risk of transmission. The world knows. There aren't enough ventilators or protective equipment for our health workers, but their risk and the risk we all face is not the product of socially created stigma. It is a consequence of government stupidity and ineptness that, buttressed by the stigmas of homosexuality and drug use, delayed government intervention for four years, not months.

I don't know what social solidarity looks like beyond the health workers. Everything is virtual. Virtual schools. Virtual shopping. Virtual happy hours. Virtual sex?

Maybe people are buying groceries for elders. Maybe transgender sex workers are being sheltered by friends. Maybe.

I wonder how we will live a year from now.

MARCH 29, 2020

Anxiety level high today as I scan the news and it's all bad. Close to 18,000 cases in NYC. I want to just curl up in bed and stay there.

SAN FRANCISCO, 1983

On January 1, 1983, in collaboration with University of California, San Francisco and San Francisco–based colleagues, Drs. Paul Volberding, Connie Wofsy, and Donald Abrams opened Ward 86, on the 6th floor of Building 80 on the San Francisco General Hospital (SFGH) campus. It became the first HIV-dedicated outpatient clinic in the country.[1] Six months later, the hospital opened Ward 5B, the first dedicated inpatient AIDS unit.

Diane Jones and Charles Cloninger were the first nurses to volunteer for duty on Ward 5B. The entire staff for the ward were volunteers. Nurses, doctors, janitors, clerks, and social workers.

At the time, Diane was a recent graduate of UCSF Nursing School. A former Peace Corps volunteer in Togo, where she met Roma Guy, Diane was no stranger to the compassion and social solidarity it would take to address the horror of AIDS in San Francisco in 1983. She had a family with Roma. She was a founder of the Women's Building. She was tall with unruly curls, easy with a laugh, always gentle. She went to nursing school to work on women's health. But Ward 5B called and she answered.

The men who first came to San Francisco emergency rooms and later to Wards 86 and 5B were dead men walking. Their families and friends abandoned them. Some in hospital beds were unwashed because staff refused to touch them. Little was understood about modes of transmission and there was no cure, no intervention that would keep these men safe or living longer. They were going to die. What Diane and the rest of the staff on Ward 5B gave them was a few days or weeks of being seen and heard, cared for, touched. It was a compassion and caring rarely found in the fear-stricken world of San Francisco in 1983. Diane continues her work on AIDS to this day.

SAN FRANCISCO, 1989

I remember Doug Warner, Rocco's lover and Marcie's best friend. I remember his blazing blue eyes, acerbic wit, and irascible, unbound energy. He snorted when annoyed or when he meant to be dismissive. He stood tall despite his diminutive height. He only went all puppy and soft for Rocco.

On a trip east to visit family, Marcie and I went to spend a couple of days with Doug's family in Peconic Bay. His mother was farm-rugged and gracious. She adored her son. When his sister showed up with two gorgeous little girls in sun hats and yellow sundresses, she kept them close to her and away from her gay brother. But she couldn't do it all day. One of the girls walked over to me and sat easy on my lap. She asked: "Are you a boy or a girl?" I replied by asking her what she thought. "Both," she said. Indeed.

AZT was introduced in 1987 as a potential intervention after a very fast and, some argued, flawed clinical trial. The early side effects included severe intestinal problems, nausea, vomiting, headaches, and anemia as the drug targeted bone marrow cells. It offered an extra year of life.

Many, including Doug, declined it. There were 40,000 AIDS-related deaths and 50,000 new cases reported in 1987. Despite AZT, recorded AIDS cases had reached over a million by 1991.

In 1989, as Doug's illness progressed, we created a make-shift hospice care unit in his living room. Feeding him. Washing him. Reading to him. Watching that effervescent energy drain from him slowly, painfully. Until it was time for Ward 5B.

At the hospital, we took turns sitting by his bed, holding his hand, watching him struggle to breathe. A thin cotton robe barely covered him, and I repeatedly bent over to cover his exposed penis. We prayed he could hold on until his mother arrived.

In a moment when he seemed to be conscious, I leaned over and whispered to him, "Please hang on," so that his mother could say goodbye. He opened those blue eyes wide and said: "Fuck off, Carmen!"

They were the last words I heard him speak. He died that night.

Marcie, March 30, 2020

SAN FRANCISCO, 1990

One way that I dealt with the shock of Doug's illness was to create a colorful "care calendar" with bright rainbow markers. Using a wall calendar decorated with cartoon characters, I carefully wrote in the names of volunteers for the many daily and weekly tasks necessary so that he would not have to leave the beloved apartment in the Castro neighborhood he had called home for decades. I took on the responsibility of organizing our friends, his current and former lovers, colleagues, and friends of friends into shifts, channeling all of my fears into a strict schedule of who was volunteering to shop, cook, clean up, launder, get him to doctors' appointments, and deliver whatever he needed or wanted in the roughly six weeks from his official Kaposi's sarcoma diagnosis in December to his death on Valentine's Day. It was my way of coping—by focusing on dates, times, tasks, I could somewhat manage my nightmares and feelings of dread and convince myself that maybe he would be the one in a million who survived.

The last time I saw him, writhing on his hospital bed in Ward 5B, he begged me to help him. There was nothing I could do except hold his hand. It was one of the worst moments of my life.

Carmen, March 31, 2020

Day 14 of quarantine is finally here. But there is nowhere to go on this raw, miserably cold day on the cape. Waiting for the sun. The estimate of 200,000 deaths from COVID-19 is making me want to run screaming until my legs can't work anymore.

SAN FRANCISCO, 1991

I remember Reggie Williams, his dreads and brilliant smile. In 1988, he and Phil Wilson founded the National Task Force on AIDS, the first and only national organization created by and for gay men of color. In an interview with John-Manuel Andriote (Victory Deferred), Reggie said of the Task Force: "If they're not going to do it [prevention for gay men of color], then goddamn it, we can do it for ourselves. We're not crippled! We have power!" Reggie understood the layers of culture, family, and religion that made mainstream messaging for gay white men irrelevant to men like himself. He said often that the "the messenger is just as important as the message." It still is.

The task force brought together Black, Latino, Asian, Pacific Islander, and Native American men. It is impossible to know how many gay men of color survived because of Reggie Williams. He died in 1996 from AIDS complications in Amsterdam, where he had gone to get away from the stigma and discrimination toward gay men with HIV/AIDS that was rampant in America and to be with his German partner Wolfgang Schreiber.

Reggie died a hero.

There was another hero from that time. There were many of them. Jesse Johnson was a Mexican/Chicano whom I loved to tease for having such a quintessentially American name. Plenty of Americans, Irish, Germans, and more stepped all over Mexico and into its women, he would say. Plenty more like him. Jesse was an AIDS prevention specialist for Proyecto Contra SIDA por Vida. His work helped save countless Latino gay men in the Bay Area.

Marcie, Late March 2020

Before we learned about the bodega a block down Third Avenue where we could buy "real" masks (rubberized cloth for $8 each from the proprietor—still open!), Anni and I improvised, using her scarf from the 2018 elections and my sleep mask from the last Jet Blue flight I took back from teaching at the University of Nevada, Las Vegas in February. It was late March and we were braving the six-block walk south on Third to Trader Joe's, one of the few grocery stores in Manhattan still open from 9:00 A.M. to 5:00 P.M. every day, to get some groceries. The governor's "Pause" order—to stay home unless absolutely necessary, and to wear masks whenever we HAD to be out in public—had been announced with great fanfare and was about to take effect. "Stay home, New York!" We were hell-bent on complying as much as possible;

the situation was frightening, getting worse daily throughout the city and state. With relatively limited testing available, New York's COVID-19 positives, and deaths, were climbing rapidly.

We were relieved to see that the TJ folks were on it: in preparation for the onslaught of shoppers, they had chalk-marked six-foot blue dividers on the pavement outside the store to control the people waiting, in a quiet line that stretched around the block about halfway to Second Avenue. We dutifully claimed our spot and waited with our little cart along with at least one hundred other people of all ages, genders, colors, shapes, and sizes.

The oddity of New Yorkers in masks waiting meekly in line on a "workday" (whatever that means now) to spend their money on basic necessities and being relatively nice to one another helped.

Inside the store, while some people disregarded the new rules of social distancing—especially around the fresh produce displays—it was every person for themselves, virus be damned!—most of us tried to be sane and decent. We even cracked macabre jokes about which treats had found their way into whose cart and why—or why the hell not!—while in line to check out. Traveling home along normally loud and crazy-busy streets, where traffic was so slight you could just cross whether you had the "Walk" sign or not, was eerie. The streets were deserted. And depressing.

Again, I was reminded of the ways in which the HIV/AIDS epidemic affected public life in San Francisco in the 1980s and '90s. Going from glitter to grim seemingly overnight, the Castro gayborhood increasingly looked and felt like a sad waiting room for dying men, who had once bounced down its sidewalks and hung out in its bars and cafes laughing, flirting, yelling over the always constantly blaring disco music. Increasingly, the vibrancy of the streets was replaced by a quiet dread and the impulse not to lift your eyes from the ground so as not to look at anyone. The fear that you would not be able to fix your face from reflecting the horror if you happened to meet someone you knew—but didn't know was "sick"—was always there. Then, as now, small businesses shut down or transformed into managing the disease in whatever way possible. And the streets fell silent—until they didn't. We also organized, resisted, protested, and did what we could to insist that the authorities pay attention. Now. Do something!

Carmen, April 3, 2020

More rain and howling winds. Might as well be in the Arctic. I am heartsick for my sister and niece and my grand-nephew, who are stuck in a completely red zone in Brooklyn. I can't bring them here because it's not my house and its owners are afraid to bring anyone else up. I am distraught. I hang in the balance between rage at not being able to protect my loved ones and gratitude for the safe place where I'm staying. I chafe at my privilege. I want to go home, and I know that my choices are limited. Go back to the COVID-19 epicenter, or stay. I am staying, hoping not to internalize the rage and shame I feel.

APRIL 7

The sun returned and with it the beach, which has blessed me with soft sand and gentle waves and the smell of salt and seaweed.

APRIL 8

Reading of others who are remembering the AIDS pandemic in the '80s and '90s. Many think that HIV/AIDS is something in the past. It isn't. More that 675,000 have died of

HIV/AIDS in the United States since the beginning of the HIV pandemic. In the United States, nearly 13,000 die each year.[2] Globally, 75 million people have been infected with the HIV virus and 32 million have died. In 2018, 44 million people were living with HIV (WHO 2020). So why does the world shrug at HIV/AIDS?

Some science explains why. HIV is sexually transmitted, or blood borne. COVID-19 is airborne. During the AIDS epidemic in the United States, the LGBTQ+ community and its allies came together to nurture those in need, to fight for prevention and treatment in a massive mobilization led by ACT UP, to mourn together. COVID-19 sends us flying from each other and into isolation.

Then there are the social diseases: homophobia, sexism, xenophobia, racism, poverty. The lives and deaths of gay men, drug users, sex workers, Haitians, Asians, and Africans mattered less then and now. Before this is over, it will be garbage collectors, bus and train drivers, police and firefighters, grocery store workers, utility workers, and our frontline health care workers who will count most prominently among the dead. The current political leadership doesn't care about the old, the poor, or people of color any more than they cared about gay men. They never have.

APRIL 9

My sister Ida's nurse called to tell me Ida was on her way to the hospital with a fever of 103 degrees. I thought my heart would burst. She lives in Buda, TX, about 35 minutes from my brother Eric in Austin. He died on October 9, 2019, and I couldn't bear losing another sibling. She went to the hospital with a fever but was instead sent home at 4:00 P.M. that afternoon because she wasn't "critical" enough. I raged at God, the Universe, and fucking COVID.

The beach offered no solace today. I sat on the sand and cried.

APRIL 10

Ida got her test today thanks to the kindness of her caretaker, Rosario, who has been with her every day for the last two months. Rosario is a Mexican woman raising a child with Down syndrome. Her physical and spiritual strength are a lifeline to her daughter and my sister. She laughs. She cleans and gets the groceries. She takes Ida to the doctor. She calls George, Ida's cat, Gordo.

Andale, Rosario. You are what heroes are made of.

Now we wait for the test results.

APRIL 13

Ida's test for COVID 19 came back negative.

MAY 27

What happened to the last two weeks?

Anxiety made my skin weep. A crawling, sick, brick neck, back-clutching anxiety. A twelve-year-old on the verge of puberty venting her hormones and screaming at her parents. Her sounds penetrated my heart like a knife wound. Sleepless nights. The front page of last Sunday's *New York Times* filled with the names of a thousand dead harking back to the *Bay Area Reporter*'s weeks and months and years of naming those claimed by AIDS. Black men being murdered by white racists in Georgia, by police in Minnesota. The deranged and despicable man in the White House flinging insults and conspiracy theories to the media because he can't lead or live in his own bloated skin without the constant drumming of lies while he is whisked off to golf, mask-less. He hopes to distract us from the 100,000 and more lives he has and will continue to sacrifice. . . .

But we will not forget.

I have taken comfort in books and walks and the song of birds during this burgeoning spring in Woods Hole: "Baltimore Orioles," robins and cardinals, sparrows and crows and osprey. I have watched seagulls and hawks sunbathing on rocks in the ocean. Somehow, I have made it back to my computer and a blank page that didn't frighten me.

WASHINGTON, DC, 1987

Since Washington wasn't seeing or hearing us, we went to Washington to be seen in our full queer splendor and to be heard—loudly.

The 1987 March on Washington for Lesbian and Gay Rights was the largest gathering of LGBTQ people in the United States at that time, drawing 300,000 participants. There was civil disobedience in front of the Supreme Court. There was a protest for marriage equality and a mass "wedding" in front of the Treasury. There was the first national viewing of the AIDS Memorial Quilt. There was lobbying for AIDS prevention and treatment.

So many smart, funny, courageous queer and queer-supporting people all over Washington, DC. The three national co-chairs of the march: Pat Norman, Steve Ault, and Kay Osberg. Also there: Cleve Jones, Ginny Apuzzo, A. S. Billy Jones, and Frank Kameny. Joan Biren with her omnipresent camera slung around her neck capturing the march and attendant events for generations to come. Marcie Gallo and yours truly! Whoopi Goldberg, Jesse Jackson, and Cesar Chavez spoke.

Getting on and off the metro was a jolt of joy. On the escalators we passed literally hundreds of men and women with their arms wrapped around each other—shouting, prancing, singing.

I remember the National AIDS Memorial Quilt display most of all. There were 1,920 panels naming those lost, the joy and briefness of their lives, the sorrow of those who mourned them. It covered the Mall in front of the Washington Memorial, and I saw gay couples, parents and children and friends of those now gone holding onto each other. Or kneeling on the ground, weeping.

Marcie and I participated in the marriage equality demonstration in front of the Treasury. It was a mass wedding that we dubbed the "Moonie Wedding" (as per the mass weddings conducted by the Reverend Moon). A reporter from the Bay Area interviewed us and two young gay men. He asked, "Why are you doing this?" Marcie and I expounded on the principles of equality and civil rights for all, etc. The young men responded in swoony sing song: "Because we're in love!" Marcie's brother Ed, her brother Michael, and his wife Shelley greeted us at the hotel to congratulate us on the wedding with bottles of Cold Duck. Cold Duck!

MAY 28

Larry Kramer died yesterday. The Normal Heart beats no more. He wasn't my favorite queer celebrity, but God, he made a difference in the landscape of AIDS.

Thank you and rest in peace, Larry.

Marcie, May 29, 2020

This is the only way I feel safe these days, "going full terrarium" in my small one-bedroom apartment in the middle of Manhattan. Shared with my spouse, my love, my best friend Anni, it provides a sense of safety and security that is now fraying at the seams.

For me, despite (or perhaps because of) the demands to "reopen" by Covidiots, who are armed to the teeth and spitting in the faces of cops at city and state legislatures throughout the nation, safety continues to require staying home unless I am carefully venturing out.

My routine has evolved into leaving our haven feeling as fully protected as possible, with mask/hat/sunglasses/sneakers, all carefully discarded at the front door upon return and segregated from the rest of the dirty clothes. All this for a one- or two-hour walk once or twice a week. We still are not sure exactly how many ways this strange new virus can be transmitted, so extreme caution feels necessary. We know that personal contact can be dangerous outside one's "hub." Another reminder of the early days, months, years of HIV/AIDS, when people were afraid to touch, or hug, or kiss a loved one, until we learned that this is not how the virus is spread.

The other weekly outdoor adventure, demanding the same suit-up and strip-down routine, is shopping for groceries on Sundays before 8:00 A.M. during "Senior Hour" at the local Trader Joe's. What a contrast to our priorities during the AIDS years, when groceries definitely took a backseat to cocktails, wine, and weed.

The rest of the time is spent here at home, cooking, cleaning, doing yoga and virtual workouts, checking my email and Twitter, watching TV—selectively. But even careful involvement with television or internet news means reckoning with not only the previously inconceivable, yet all too real, hundred thousand dead from COVID-19 but also the increasing horrors of police and white supremacist violence against Black men and women, young, middle-aged, old, caught by out-of-control killers while jogging, shopping, or sleeping in their own homes, harming no one. Yet another epidemic, a particularly American one, an epidemic of racial violence that is centuries old and inflamed by hateful rhetoric from bogus and corrupt "leaders."

It is making me sick, in my heart, soul, and psyche.

Harvey Milk. Exuberant. Jew. Former New Yorker. Mayor of Castro Street. Slayer of Briggs. Ran a "Scoop the Poop" campaign for which he got mega media attention that may well have finally gotten him elected to the San Francisco Board of Supervisors in November 1977. It was a heady, delirious time to be queer in San Francisco.

And two years earlier there was delirium among the supporters of the wholesome and handsome Elaine Noble, elected to the Massachusetts State Legislature in 1975. She was the first openly lesbian or gay person elected to a state legislature in American history.

We were celebrating, moving the forces of justice and liberation forward from coast to coast. We could not yet see the dark storms heading our way—the political storms, the viral storm, and how they would come together to kill thousands of us.

The right was frothing, convulsed. The "Homosexual Agenda" was upending the American way of life. Homosexuals were being elected to political office!

We were a menace that had to be eradicated!

In 1977, in Dade County, Florida, Anita Bryant launched the Save Our Children Campaign in response to the adoption of an ordinance prohibiting discrimination on the basis of sexual orientation. The ordinance was overturned, which led to organized opposition to gay rights that spread across the country through the involvement of televangelist Jerry Falwell. During the campaign Bryant said: "as a mother, I know that homosexuals cannot biologically reproduce children; therefore, they must recruit our children," and "If gays are granted rights, then we'll have to give them to prostitutes and people who sleep with Saint Bernards and to nail biters." Her success led to several other campaigns across the country and to the Briggs Initiative in California, which would have made pro-gay statements regarding homosexual people or homosexuality in the school system grounds for dismissal.

It was against this backdrop that Harvey Milk's election was celebrated. He famously debated former California state senator John Briggs in September 1978 and shredded his arguments to pieces. He campaigned throughout California against the Briggs Initiative and, buoyed by an extraordinary grassroots campaign, it lost by more than a million votes.

I didn't know about Elaine Noble until much later, and what I knew of Harvey Milk was mostly from his enigmatic presence on Castro Street, light and laughter pouring out of him, glad-handing, showing off his camera shop. He was hard to resist. But I have an indelible memory of him from the Pride March and Rally in front of San Francisco's City Hall in 1978. It was the height of the campaign against the Briggs Initiative.

I had been scheduled to speak as a representative of the Stonewall Club, egged on by my friend Ali Marrero, and stood nervously behind the stage waiting my turn. Several speakers were scheduled ahead of me, including Sally Gearhart, orator extraordinaire, who introduced Harvey Milk. He bounded to the stage in a white T-shirt, jeans, and rainbow suspenders, flashing that brilliant smile and waving for what seemed like an eternity before the roars of the crowd quieted enough for him to speak. He spoke of courage in the face of bigotry. He spoke of protecting gay youth and gay teachers and democracy writ large. He bounded off the stage to more roars and I was introduced. I threw my notes away. I have no idea what I said.

Clearly, there was a social and political life in San Francisco before AIDS.

Between 1971 and 1981, when the full horror of AIDS began unveiling itself, there was a frenzy of social and political activism and community organizing that laid the foundation for what would become the fight back against AIDS by San Francisco's queer activists. José Saria and the Society for Individual Rights; Phyllis Lyon and Del Martin and the Daughters of Bilitis; Harvey Milk, Anne Kronenburg, Harry Britt. Billy Jones. Roma Guy and Diane Jones and the Women's Building. The White Night riots. Donna Hichens and Roberta Achtenberg and the National Center for Lesbian Rights. The Stonewall Democratic Club. The Alice B. Toklas Democratic Club. Carol Migden and the Operation Concern Club. The GALA (Gay Latino Alliance). The Gay Asian Pacific Alliance. The Sisters of Perpetual Indulgence. Some were radical, some conservative. Some were serious political activists, others service providers. Some were just for fun. Ultimately, they came together in grief and with courage to tend to the dying and fight back against government indifference to HIV/AIDS.

I left San Francisco in October 1978 and returned in January 1979 to a city somber and still in mourning over the Milk and Moscone murders. AIDS was still a year away.

Marcie, June 30, 2020

This year's alternative Pride celebration in New York captured the intensity and anger of this moment and our movements for justice. I am so glad to have been a part of it.

In spite of our continuing reluctance to spend time—even outdoors—in groups, Anni and I decided to take part in the Silent Vigil organized for the beginning of the day's march from Foley Square to Washington Square Park. Each one of the more than four dozen people stood for thirty minutes of visual testimony, holding signs with the names of too many Black people killed by hate and white supremacy over the years.

Carmen, June 30, 2020

I can't breathe. I can't breathe. I can't breathe. I can't breathe.

Eric Garner. George Floyd. How many others? The posters are ubiquitous. The faces of Black men killed by police stare blankly over the thousands who protest in their names. I hold my breath for 30 seconds, trying to imagine what it might feel like to have my neck in a choke hold or under the knee of a strong man, and my heart wants to explode.

But this didn't begin with George Floyd or Eric Garner. The grief and rage of Black Americans began more than 400 years ago in the British colony of Jamestown, Virginia, where four African slaves were sold by Portuguese pirates to English colonists.

The rage is for African slaves who had children ripped from them, for African slaves who were chained, beaten, hanged and burned. The rage is for Black men who were lynched for supposedly looking at white women. The rage is for Black women who were raped because their masters could do it with impunity.

It may no longer be a noose, but whether by a gun or a knee or a beating to death, the lynching of Black men continues. The sexual debasement of Black women has not ended. Slave houses may no longer exist, but prisons do, with a national ratio of imprisonment for Black people that is five times higher than that of white people.

The "Liberty and Justice for All" clarion call of our Declaration of Independence did not include Black people. The original Constitution of the United States did not count Black people as full humans.

The soon-to-be-celebrated 244th anniversary of the Declaration of Independence from British tyranny enacted by the original 13 colonies was writ with the blood and forced labor of enslaved Africans. It was writ with the forced removal and death by violence or disease of the Indigenous people of this land. It was written by white, property-owning men whose wives and daughters too often were rendered silent, complicit, by vaunted racist rhetoric.

Don't ask me to celebrate that. America's original sins of slavery and Native American genocide have flowed through the veins of white Americans and into the skin of their children for more than 244 years, fueling the death by violence of thousands from Jamestown to Wounded Knee to the Alamo to Tulsa to New York to Minneapolis.

I can't celebrate that.

And yet, America is also the country of Nat Turner's slave rebellion and countless rebellions before and after him, of Sojourner Truth, who did not say "Ain't I a Woman?" but did say: "But man is in a tight place, the poor slave is on him, woman is coming on him, and he is surely between—a hawk and a buzzard."

America is the country of Harriet Tubman and the Underground Railroad, of Frederick Douglass and Langston Hughes, Bessie Smith, Zora Neil Hurston, Audre Lorde, and James Baldwin. America is the country of Black women and men who served in World War II. America is the country of Thurgood Marshall, Martin Luther King Jr., and Bayard Rustin. America belongs to the tennis courts of Althea Gibson and Serena Williams; it belongs to Colin Kaepernick, who took a knee at the playing of the National Anthem to protest police brutality and has inspired thousands who now kneel on their own knees. America belongs to Little Richard and Prince, to Lin-Manuel Miranda and Beyoncé. America is the country where queers have gone from hiding in bars and suffering electroshock therapy and the death of thousands to AIDS to marriage equality and equality in the workplace. America belongs to Shirley Chisholm and Michelle Obama, to Alexandria Ocasio-Cortez, Tammy Duckworth, and Ilhan Omar.

America is the country where thousands of white Americans have joined with Black Lives Matter and people of color in protest of police violence and the disproportionate share of COVID-19 deaths among people of color, and perhaps, on the road to a reconciliation over 400 years in the making.

I will celebrate that America.

Marcie, January 27, 2021

Got a call from Carmen's sister Ida tonight.

Barely audible through her sobs, I heard the words "Carmen's dead."

"No, no, no," I whispered, clutching the phone to my ear and rocking forward on my knees.

No, it cannot be true. No, please God, no.

But it was.

Just two weeks after her seventy-second birthday, twelve long and frightening days after she was taken to the intensive care unit at NYU Langone in Brooklyn, with a high fever and unable to breathe on her own, my dear friend was taken by COVID-19. She faced too many uphill battles because of serious underlying health problems.

Today I am both grateful and haunted by having seen Carmen two weeks earlier, on January 11, 2021, for the first time since our dinner party the year before. She had returned to New York in December to begin consultation and treatment for a medical issue, and her doctor's appointment in January was scheduled at an office near our apartment.

She was not feeling well when she arrived and could barely eat the meal we had prepared for her to celebrate her birthday. She slept on our couch for most of the afternoon and then left to return to her sister's home in Brooklyn, where she was living temporarily.

It was the last time I saw her.

A few days later she was admitted to the hospital in the intensive care unit, and the emotional roller coaster of fear and hope began. For the next two weeks, I was in what felt like constant contact with Carmen's sisters, Nancy and Ida. Her friend Carlie, who had her health proxy, arrived from Massachusetts and took up residence at the hospital.

No visitors allowed.

Anni and I turned to family and close friends who are medical professionals to learn what we could expect after she had been intubated and placed on a ventilator. There were many moments of intense worry and some signs, few and fleeting, of improvement.

But the virus was too strong and her body too weak.

Afterwards, what felt like hundreds of phone calls, emails, and text messages flooded in from family, friends, and colleagues (both those still close and others who seemingly were long-lost) as we shared the news and tried to provide one another some solace. Carmen's niece Nicole began to organize a family memorial via Zoom and folks at the Woodhull Freedom Foundation planned a "movement" memorial, both held within two months of Carmen's passing.

I searched through boxes of journals, photographs, and other mementos of our years as partners and friends, selecting images to contribute to the PowerPoint shows for each memorial.

She and Anni and me at a Yankees game. Carmen at the beach with my family. Marching together with ACLU and Somos Hermanas. A goodbye picnic at our home in

Marcie Gallo and Carmen Vázquez, 2012. (Courtesy of Marcie Gallo. Photograph by Ann Cammett.)

Berkeley before we moved to New York. Happy memories to counteract the despair.

The loss is enormous—for me, her family and friends, and for the many movements for equality, justice, and joy that she embraced. May her memory be a revolution.

POSTSCRIPT

Carmen succumbed to complications from COVID-19 on January 27, 2021. The tragedy of losing her to COVID echoes the intense pain of losing my best friend Doug to AIDS in 1990. Both losses make very real for me the personal costs of both pandemics.

I am grateful that Carmen and I took time this past year to share our remembrances of some of the heartaches and fear—as well as the love and resilience—of our years in San Francisco. Writing about our past from our different perspectives and locations expanded our involvement in one another's lives during a time of isolation and quarantine, and it brought to the surface decades-old memories that gave us hope and some happiness in times of despair. She was excited about the possibility of sharing our writings publicly. Although it has been difficult—at times nearly impossible—for me to return to them and complete the project we started, I do so to honor Carmen, her brilliance and passion, and to remember and lift up all those whom we have lost.

Editors' Note

Carmen was a participant in IRW's 2018–2019 Distinguished Lecture Series, where she spoke on a panel entitled "My City Was Gone: Gentrification, AIDS, and Urban Change." She submitted an early version of this chapter for publication in this volume. We honor her memory by posthumously publishing this work. You can read her *New York Times* obituary at https://www.nytimes.com/2021/02/05/obituaries/carmen-vazquez-dead-coronavirus.html.

Notes

1. UCSF AIDS Research Institute, "Ward 86," https://ari.ucsf.edu/clinical-care/ward-86.

    An excellent documentary about the first AIDS ward in the United States, *5B*, is available at: https://tubitv.com/movies/552763/5b?start=true&tracking=google-feed&utm_source=google-feed.

2. See the Centers for Disease Control and Prevention's statistics on HIV/AIDS, which can be accessed on NCHHSTP Atlas-Plus. https://www.cdc.gov/nchhstp/about/atlasplus.html.

References

Brier, Jennifer. 2020. "We Can't Forget Women as We Tell the Story of COVID-19." *Washington Post*, March 12, 2020. https://www.washingtonpost.com/outlook/2020/03/12/we-cant-forget-women-we-tell-story-covid-19/.

Bronski, Michael. 2020. "Fighting for Public Health." *Boston Review*, April 1, 2020. https://bostonreview.net/articles/michael-bronski-bronski/.

Farrow, Kenyon. 2020. "Lessons from the AIDS Epidemic for COVID-19" (interview transcript). *The Laura Flanders Show*, March 19, 2020. https://lauraflanders.org/2020/03/kenyon-farrow-lessons-from-the-aids-epidemic-for-covid-19-full-interview/.

Fong, Kevin. 2020. "Love in the Time of Coronavirus: What Living Through the HIV/AIDS Epidemic Taught Me." *Yes! Magazine*, March 18, 2020. https://www.yesmagazine.org/opinion/2020/03/18/coronavirus-hiv-aids-epidemic.

Rodriguez, Mathew. "COVID-19 and HIV Are Not the Same. But They're Similar in Many Ways That Matter." *The Body*, April 9, 2020. https://www.thebody.com/article/covid-19-aids-not-same-but-similar-in-many-ways?fbclid=IwAR0WKTPPP5Vfs0zgCb2jaxmsUBIEadJ8jIGC_8lyY0MuNP-Mpho6Lo875-8.

Schulman, Sarah. 2021. *Let the Record Show: A Political History of ACT UP New York, 1987–1993.* New York: Farrar, Strauss, and Giroux.

United Nations. 2020. "Policy Brief: The Impact of COVID-19 On Women." April 9, 2020. https://www.unwomen.org/sites/default/files/Headquarters/Attachments/Sections/Library/Publications/2020/Policy-brief-The-impact-of-COVID-19-on-women-en.pdf.

Weston, Kath. 1997. *Families We Choose: Lesbians, Gays, Kinship.* New York: Columbia University Press.

Wilder, Terri. 2021. "LGBTQ Activists Remember Carmen Vázquez." *The Body*, February 24, 2021. https://www.thebody.com/article/carmen-vazquez-lgbtq-activist.

World Health Organization (WHO). 2020. "HIV/AIDS." Archived April 19, 2020, at the Wayback Machine. https://web.archive.org/web/20200419022243/https://www.who.int/data/gho/data/themes/hiv-aids.

5

Skin and Screen

A Collaborative Take on Touch in the Time of COVID

KATHLEEN C. RILEY, SMRUTHI BALA KANNAN,
STACY S. KLEIN, ELLEN MALENAS LEDOUX,
BASULI DEB, AND L. AMEDE OBIORA

Introduction

KATHLEEN C. RILEY

In September 2020, a group of scholars came together for the IRW Seminar at Rutgers University. We were there to discuss our research on the fluidity of sexual bodies, but by the end of the academic year we realized that we had been thinking and talking about more than our research problems. Some were juggling computer-mediated professional obligations with full-time caregiving for young children; others were struggling to manage medical vulnerabilities as well as technological constraints. But all of us were deeply aware that something socially significant had emerged from our weekly attempts to communicate via Zoom.

So, during the last session of the year, six of us decided that we wanted to devote some time to writing collaboratively about the complexities of skin and screen as we had experienced them. These two surfaces had become newly entangled due to the world-altering health crisis: the skin, a permeable boundary between self and other, and the screen, a two-dimensional conduit for continued sociality and "staying in touch." The following piece is the result of that endeavor.

What we have tried to do is draw upon our personal experiences and our academic disciplines to reflect on how the pandemic affected our relationships to children, students, colleagues, and strangers. We also explore how technology transformed domestic settings and professional venues. Even as we explore our individual difficulties (from Zoom fatigue to the loss of sensory stimuli), all of us are aware of the extreme inequities experienced by so many throughout the world due to the viral toll, the digital divide, and the economic consequences of the total shutdown of the economy. Our collaboration reveals a growing foreboding about the vulnerability of our bodies, neighborhoods, and planet. Through our reflections, we wish to join forces with those who are "staying with the trouble" (Haraway 2016), learning the "arts of living on a damaged planet" (Tsing et al. 2017), and finding new ways to care (*Anthropology News* 2021).

Storyboard, Incomplete

SMRUTHI BALA KANNAN

1. We played for a bit after our IRW meeting one Thursday.
2. We experimented with changing our backgrounds.
3. We were making sense of the screen through the skin and the skin through the screen.

WE PLAYED FOR A BIT

AFTER OUR IRW SESSION ONE THURSDAY

4. I appeared and dissolved into the background as the screen tried to distinguish skin from wall, cupboard, shadows, books, and sun.

5. I shifted between rooms, cities, and countries, with varying internet bandwidths, always sitting on the floor with my lap desk, always trying to connect.

6. "Can you hear me okay?" Only my voice mattered. I could switch the video off.

7. It had been decades since primary school, when I sat on the floor to participate in a class.
8. I had not thought much about how the skin on my feet felt when I was with others in a seminar or a class.
9. My skin had been enclosed in a shoe or a slipper at least, under the table. Out of sight, out of mind.
10. During this seminar, I felt cold floor, warm mat, a cockroach under the desk, glass broken on the floor, cozy on a pillow, itchy, oiled, cramped, stretched, anklets on and tapping a beat, my feet shifted and twisted during these meetings.
11. You could not see parts of my skin, not because I covered it with a shoe or a jacket—but because I was elsewhere even when we were together.

———————

Cases of dry eye and other eye ailments increase as screen light touches our eyes over and over again. What load does the liberation from ones' other bodily demands place on the liquid layers of the cornea? To be thrilled to perceive and connect using our eyes: Is this a privileging of vision over the eye's tactile materialities? When I interviewed Ayurveda and Siddha physicians and healers in 2019, they raised concerns over children's screen time, stating that any source of light such as a TV screen, computer, or phone is simultaneously a source that stimulates *dryness* and *heat* in the human body. They were also worried by inactivity due to extended screen time, which enables the retention of *damp* and *cold*. I am fascinated to think about the screen as a source rather than a regulator of heat.

As I join you in the liberation that the screen affords to my skin, I also worry for my eyes. I wonder why I am among others who are structurally in a position to celebrate the masking and privacy of our skins.

Terms of the Pandemic

STACY S. KLEIN

The grinding work of co-existing with COVID-19 has focused unprecedented attention on both "skin" and "screen," so that I find myself considering the historical, literary, and lexical dimensions of these terms. The word "skin" is derived from the Old Norse *skinn* ("animal hide" or "fur") and is closely related to the Dutch *schinden* and German *schinden* ("to flay, peel")—an etymology that gestures toward the violence inflicted upon certain bodies forced to serve others (*Oxford English Dictionary Online*, n.d.b.). For centuries, Western societies transmitted and preserved much of their written culture on the skin of animals (Holsinger 2009).[1] My work as a medievalist has given me a deep ambivalence toward skin: it is both the medium that has enabled the survival of the beautiful texts that I study and an ever-present reminder that my scholarship is founded on the deaths of innumerable sheep, lambs, calves, and goats, whose lives were cut short for the production of books.[2]

There is something visceral and almost sacred about literature recorded in this manner: blood sacrifice had to occur for it to come into being. Medieval manuscripts remind modern readers of this sense of enchantment. To hold a thousand-year-old manuscript is to feel skin's power to make connections that might be otherwise impossible—in this case, a touch with the past or even a brush with divinity.

Throughout both the Middle Ages and the pandemic, skin could be idealized as a crucial component of our shared humanity as well as a tool for transcending it. Medieval saints and monastics embraced hair shirts, self-flagellation, and stigmata to imitate Christ's suffering, while during the days of the pandemic, loneliness was often expressed as a longing for human touch. The climate of enforced insularity imposed by COVID-19 prompted difficult questions: Could we live with such severe restrictions on human contact, and if so, what kind of life might this be?

The anonymous Old English elegy *The Wanderer* (ca. 960–980 A.D.) depicts a drifting "solitary one" or *anhaga*, bereft of community and earthly comforts. When the wanderer falls asleep, his dream centers on a happier time, characterized exclusively by an abundance of touch: "when sorrow and sleep both together / often bind the wretched solitary man; / it seems to him in his mind that he embraces and kisses / his [war]lord, and on his knees might lay / hands and head."[3] Human touch in *The Wanderer* functions as a synecdoche for numerous aspects of the social world, including friends, kinfolk, communal feasting, gift-giving, political rule, and even civilization itself.

The symbolic capaciousness of touch resonates, almost a millennium later, in Eugene O'Neill's play of masks, *The Great God Brown* (1926). Overwhelmed by familial expectations and artistic aspirations, and unable to reciprocate the affections of a young infatuated Margaret, the protagonist Dion Anthony slowly lifts his head, takes off his mask, and laments: "Why am I afraid to live, I who love life and the beauty of flesh and the living colors of earth and sky and sea? [. . .] Why was I born without a skin, O God, that I must wear armor in order to touch or to be touched?" (O'Neill 1926, 20). O'Neill's reflections on a life devoid of skin and shielded from touch resonates powerfully with mass fears generated by the coronavirus crisis. Faced with the terrifying possibility that the absence of skin and touch might signal the loss of our shared humanity, many people turned to the screen.

The term "screen" is slightly newer than "skin." It dates to the mid-fourteenth century, and originally referred to an upright piece of furniture designed to shield people from the direct heat of a fire or the chill of drafts. The idea of the screen as a flat vertical surface for the reception of images did not come into use until approximately 1810, when it began appearing in descriptions of magic lantern shows (*Oxford English Dictionary Online*, n.d.a.). The etymology of the term "screen" focuses attention on its protective, even magical qualities. These qualities served me well during the pandemic. While I was isolated and trapped at home with two young children, ages two and seven, screens offered a degree of protection from the panic engendered by overly full hospitals and rising death counts. Screens also offered an escape from the grueling monotony of days that bled into one another and that seemed to stretch on forever.

Best of all, the screen enabled us a temporary escape from ourselves. One of the ugliest aspects of the pandemic was that it left us alone with ourselves, forcing us to gaze incessantly upon our own lives, as well as on those with whom we shared our tiny "bubble." Such close scrutiny was rarely flattering, throwing our own personal flaws into harsh relief. Far more appealing was the possibility of inhabiting the lives of others. Reading fiction on page or screen allowed for "empathy for people we've never met, living lives we couldn't possibly experience for ourselves, because the book puts us inside the character's skin" (Patchett 2009). The screen was a powerful surface that promised to put us in touch with an endless supply of new people, ideas, texts, and feelings. It also opened new possibilities for sharing them.

In *Moby Dick*, Herman Melville warns that, "when beholding the tranquil beauty and brilliancy of the ocean's skin, one forgets the tiger heart that pants beneath it" ([1851] 2001, 534). Melville's contention that still waters conceal hidden dangers evokes a model of surface and depth found throughout Western literature, an arrangement that undergirds literary interpretation itself. Allegory, metaphor, symbolism, and figurative expression more generally are indebted to the belief that surfaces may be plumbed to unmask hidden meanings. This kind of interpretive work, often known as "symptomatic reading" or "close reading," is one of the many joys of studying literature.[4]

It proved particularly difficult to teach close reading during the pandemic. Many of my students lacked access to reading materials; we thus resorted to a range of other activities. We discussed the emotions elicited by different types of Old and Middle English metrical verse that I recited aloud, we paraphrased texts read prior to the pandemic, and we made lists and drew pictures of heroes and heroines from courtly romances. At times, the class felt overly relaxed, based on more literary appreciation than analysis, but perhaps this kind of engagement with affect, description, summary, and literary patterns, I rationalized, fell under the rubric of "surface reading" (Best and Marcus 2009). Such a practice might, as feminist scholars argue, help us replace a violent and masculinist hermeneutics of penetration with more ethical modes of analysis rooted in attention, appreciation, and care (Love 2010).

Pedagogies that prioritize care seemed particularly appropriate for teaching during the pandemic. Everyone seemed needy, and as my caregiving duties burgeoned, I began to imagine myself as a kind of essential worker for my own family and students, a local superhero whose special power resided in a highly developed capacity for multitasking. I recall one day in early April when I was genuinely convinced that, given the right amount of planning, I could synchronize my two-year-old daughter's nap and kindergarten-age son's homeschooling with the rhythms of my Zoom lecture on medieval court literature. That day nearly broke me.

In spite of their many needs, I never resented my students during the pandemic. On the contrary, I felt especially close to them during this period. International crisis seemed to prompt much local good will as well as an opportunity to re-commit to our shared academic mission. One of my students, who had returned to Beijing at the beginning of the pandemic, posted a cheery note on our classroom chat: "Hey everyone, I'm just about done with my *Beowulf* paper and so once I get used to the time difference, I should be back in class." Beijing is thirteen hours ahead of Eastern Standard Time. Keeping this promise would have entailed waking up at 2 A.M. to discuss medieval literature. I was deeply moved by Ming's herculean intentions and quick to embrace them as an affirmation that reading, writing, and creative work still mattered—even, and perhaps especially, in the midst of crisis.

Yet the truth is that I never saw Ming again. I don't know if he finished his degree or ever returned to the United States. The close-knit bonds I had imagined between myself and my students, forged over shared struggle, in the end proved no match for the personal, social, and institutional pressures of living and learning under COVID. As I was unable to "read" my students' faces and body language in person and limited to interactions mediated by unstable signals and two-dimensional screens, the pedagogical connections that felt so strong were, in fact, fragile and fleeting. The gravest danger occasioned by virtual instruction was not that faculty were barred from literally touching their students—I doubt that many instructors do this much anyway—but rather that it was easy for them to "lose touch" with their students, particularly with international students such as Ming.

The etymologies of "skin" and "screen" take us across a geographical expanse that includes Iceland, England, Denmark, Germany, France, and the Netherlands. In doing so, these terms quietly underscore the multilingual complexity of the English language and, by extension, the interconnectedness of our world. It would be an excellent thing if the pandemic might help us to recognize, honor, and nurture these global connections, so evident at the level of language, in order that they might become a more tangible part of our modern lives instead of remaining a relic of historical linguistics and the medieval past.

Privilege, Parenting, and Screens: Navigating Competing Priorities during the COVID Crisis

ELLEN MALENAS LEDOUX

They told us the suspension of face-to-face learning due to COVID-19 would be for two weeks. Looking back over my emails from this period, it appears I took the news in stride. I cobbled together discussion forums for my classes, submitted recommendation letters for former students, scheduled Zoom meetings for committee work, and even exchanged research with peers. Then came the blow that would teach me professional and personal humility. On March 13, 2020, our local public school closed, and would not re-open for in-person instruction until April 2021. My campus and department would not offer in-person instruction again until September 2021. Thus began our family's fraught relationship with the screen. It was also the moment when I experienced firsthand an argument I had made for years: "work-life balance" is a sham promulgated by those privileged enough to have access to reliable, high-quality childcare.

I am interested in this moment for both practical and intellectual reasons. I am writing a book about working mothers in the eighteenth century and curious about how these mothers managed the so-called work-life balance. Many eighteenth-century women performed amazing artistic feats or worked long hours while being perpetually pregnant and nursing in an era that pre-dates birth control or safe, legal abortion. The concerns these women voiced are similar to those expressed by many working mothers today. For example, philosopher and novelist Mary Wollstonecraft complained to her partner throughout 1794 and 1795 about the difficulty of concentrating on intellectual work while enduring the physical demands of breastfeeding (2003, 266–267, 276, 280–281). Yet, remarkably, these women managed without the contemporary advantages that modern women enjoy, including the technology that connects us to and sometimes "babysits" our kids.

During the pandemic lockdown there was no childcare. Gone were the drive-through meals hastily picked up after sports practice and other markers of our harried, overscheduled lives. Instead, I became like the women of early America, who, as Nora Doyle explains, "spent their days balancing the demands of domestic work and other labor," their cares, according to one woman, "never ceasing" (2018, 2). Did the screen provide a solution to the problems we were facing during this crisis, during which I had to teach (and write and respond to emails) and my child had to learn (and be fed and parented) simultaneously? Sometimes I found myself guiltily handing over an iPad and allowing my daughter to watch YouTube while those emails and articles got addressed. This extra screen time did not improve our lives. My daughter has a moderate form of ADHD that tends toward hyperactivity. It was incredibly difficult for her to sit in front of a screen to complete her coursework. There was no hands-on learning, no recess shared with other kids. On the days when I gave her another screen to "enjoy" during her recreational time, I am sure it exacerbated her symptoms. Meanwhile, I feverishly stared at my computer monitor trying to maximize this "stolen" time by completing academic work. When I scroll through pictures from that time on my phone (another screen!), I see that we took nature walks or engaged in tactile play, like French-braiding her hair or baking bread. I would like to believe that this kind of touch enabled my daughter to get through lockdown relatively unscathed. So, while the screen allows us to do important work and can, at times, be a saving grace, in our family it was imperative that it be balanced by the healing touch of skin, especially for my neurodiverse child.

Yet, my ability to engage in "healing touch" was possible because my job allows for telecommuting. Women who work in industries requiring their physical presence—including many women who perform low-income jobs—could not engage in the kind of fraught balancing act that occurred in my own household. The Kaiser Family Foundation reports that during the pandemic "One in ten working mothers with children under 18 said they quit a job due to COVID and half of this group cited school closures as one of the reasons" (Ranji et al. 2021). In the first six months of the pandemic, Latina women left the workforce "at nearly three times the rate of white women and more than four times the rate of African Americans" (Horsley 2020). Journalist Scott Horsley attributes this trend to both cultural and economic factors, citing Latinas' "traditional view of mothers as primary caregivers" and the fact that many Latina mothers work in industries that were "hammered by the pandemic" (Horsley 2020). In addition, the competing priorities of work and motherhood took a particular toll on poor women: "almost half (47%) of working mothers said they took unpaid sick leave because their child's school or daycare was closed. This rose to 65% among low-income mothers and 70% among those working part-time jobs" (Ranji et al. 2021).

My intention is to shed light on the ways in which inequality shapes our already fraught relationship between skin, screen, and parenting. As tiring as Zoom fatigue can be, one tends to forget that virtual meetings and collaborations enable caregivers to continue to parent and perform their jobs. However, most low-wage jobs cannot be performed via the screen. While a salaried employee might feel guilty for neglecting her work duties, a low-wage, hourly worker faces the very real dilemma of having to choose between going to work to support her children and leaving those children unsupervised. Although screens have clearly allowed some mothers to achieve a tenuous balance between work and parenting, many women are not so lucky. These mothers are left behind because they cannot telecommute.

The issues I raise are from the perspective of someone living in the Global North, but the pandemic is a worldwide phenomenon. While some comparatively poorer countries, such as Cambodia, have admirably outstripped their wealthier neighbors with their robust vaccination rates, access to vaccines remains unequal and global vaccine hesitancy is a persistent problem. As COVID overtakes the developing world, which experts suggest it surely will, how will women balance the need to work with the need to care for children? Here the loss of childcare networks might prove catastrophic, resulting in children left unsupervised without even a screen to act as an inadequate substitute for a minder. In addition, a mother's immediate need for work may increase the likelihood of her child's exposure to the virus. Peru, a country with a largely informal economy, has the highest death rate from COVID-19. As Jason Beaubien explains, when government shutdowns occurred most of the population was suddenly out of work and without a safety net. In such a situation, the "priority becomes having something to eat for the day, not staying at home and trying not to get the virus" (Beaubien 2021). Social distancing was a luxury many Peruvians could not afford. While we in the United States bemoan an excess of screen time, in some ways, our less wealthy neighbors suffer from a real excess of "skin time" that is placing them at greater risk for contracting the virus—a phenomenon that is particularly urgent when we consider the needs and challenges of working mothers.

COVID and Feminist Bioethics: From Touch to Untouchability

BASULI DEB

When New York City shut down for COVID-19 in March 2020, my thoughts turned to businesses in Manhattan that organize dinners, dances, and dating events. The lockdown provided a respite from the "hook-up" culture that these events foster—a fertile breeding ground for droplet-borne viruses. Event planning businesses turned to computer and phone screens to keep the show going, organizing a plethora of Zoom dating events. Advertisements for these events started showing up on Facebook, inviting people to join "friends" online with a glass of wine. It seemed that New Yorkers were being compelled to get wiser—dating now had to start with getting to know the other person.

Less than six months into the pandemic, an article by Evie Kirana and Francesca Tripodi in *The European Society for Sexual Medicine* reported that the increase in online activity under lockdown led to an increase in flirting. "People can feel sexual desire; they can feel wanted, understood, funny, special through online communication," the article's authors wrote, adding that the pandemic ushered in new potential for infidelity: "It is possible to have an online affair while the primary partner is in the same room." Lockdown also saw a surge of "cybersex, phone sex, sexting, [and] online sex parties." The use of messaging in dating apps owned by the Match Group soared by 27 percent (Kirana and Tripodi 2020).

The pandemic compels us to ask difficult questions about skin and screen to diversify our models for understanding intimacy and probe a feminist ethics of the screen. As I came across articles about how many were being affected by the lack of touch during COVID, I began to ask why touch was being idealized as comforting when so many cases of domestic violence were being reported during the pandemic? Why wasn't anyone asking how many felt safer operating from behind screens? What about those who felt safer at virtual social events? How about those to whom the workplace had become physically unsafe? What about those recovering from sexual assault?

My feminist provocations to think about the screen as a refuge need to be accompanied by reflections on how to sustain the screen as a safe space. Like all spaces, the screen is also about power and especially about how on-screen affect plays out in unequal power relationships. The positives and negatives of the screen during the pandemic compel us to ask: Who controls the technology behind the screen? What screen spaces are being created? By whom and with whose interests in mind? How will these on-screen relationships play out in real time, and what kinds of trauma and danger will they pose to some or all who are involved? These questions about interpersonal intimacies push us to think about the micropolitics of everyday life during the pandemic.

COVID-19 also raised concerns about intimacies between continents, to evoke Lisa Lowe's (2015) work. Given that both skin and screen entail fraught modes of embodied and disembodied touch, the politics of untouchability offers a useful way to read these macropolitics. In the traditional Indian caste classification, "untouchables," or outcastes, were those whose labor was considered polluting. Untouchables handled the dead, scavenged, and cleaned human waste. In purist societies the skins of the outcaste were segregated from caste-marked skins through the highly contagious virus of caste prejudice. Although "untouchability" was abolished in 1950 and is punishable by law, like racism it persists.

The current pandemic has thrown into intense relief the caste system operative between the nations of the Global

North and the Global South. Like the outcastes of the Indian caste system, the pandemic quickly birthed a new class of untouchables. The vaccine-starved populations of the southern countries, dependent on the wealthier North for vaccine equity, are experiencing a new form of segregation.

In a December 2021 article in the science journal *Nature*, Msomi et al. pled for vaccine equity for Africa. The article highlights how "Africa is being completely left behind as COVID-19 diagnostics, therapeutics and vaccines are deployed throughout much of the rest of the world. By mid-November [2021], more than 40% of people globally had been fully vaccinated. In Africa, it was less than 7%." Given that immunosuppressed cancer patients receiving chemotherapy and those with advanced, uncontrolled HIV are susceptible to prolonged COVID infections, the authors assert that if the COVID-19 and HIV treatment gaps in Africa are not bridged, global control of the pandemic will be difficult. When Africans have died en masse in the past, the world has stood by and watched. The Rwandan genocide of the 1990s is a well-known example, and it is happening again (Msomi et al. 2021).

The latest expression of this new North-South caste system came in the form of the 2021 travel ban on South Africa and its neighboring countries, following South African scientists' discovery of the Omicron variant. Rather than expressing thanks, the European Union, United States, and United Kingdom imposed immediate travel restrictions, thus transforming South Africans into the new untouchables. In a statement that invoked the colonial past and its connections to the wealthy nations of the North, the South African foreign affairs ministry stated: "This latest round of travel bans is akin to punishing South Africa for its advanced genomic sequencing and the ability to detect new variants quicker." The travel ban inevitably discourages scientific cooperation across borders as it dissuades the scientific community from sharing crucial information about the pandemic. Msomi et al. (2021) have urged the international community not to stigmatize South Africa for Omicron.

This discussion highlights the necessity of submitting the ethics of touch to much more discursive attention in feminist studies. Touch in its benign form communicates acceptance as the basis of relationality. However, closed borders and vaccine inequity for the untouchables do not sit well with a pandemic that makes it imperative to protect all to stop the spread of contagion.

The Personal Is Professional (Is Political) during the Pandemic

KATHLEEN C. RILEY

As a linguistic anthropologist, I became attentive early on in the pandemic to what could or could not be communicated through the screen. I was intrigued to analyze what was lost and what, if anything, gained due to the minimizing of certain sensory stimuli and the exaggeration of other modes of communication.

Confined in our separate corners, sight and hearing came to the forefront as we sought to adjust technology to clarify sounds and visuals. Taste and smell evaporated (virtually, as well as biologically) in ways that brought them more intensely to consciousness ("I wish you could taste this amazing bread I baked today, or at least smell it" . . . photo included). Additionally, we mimed relational touch and experienced it through gesture and memory.

I found myself asking survey-style questions of any interlocutor I happened to Zoom with. How does it feel to share a drink or meal together electronically? Is it worrisome to see the food being masticated or easier to imagine how the other's wine tastes like blackberry or pepper? What role does co-presence play in moving our bodies as we dance "together," or does music alone do the trick? Does the rectangle of the computer constrain us, or does it instead provide interesting formal boundaries within which we can play with our potential for relationship? Can you look into someone else's eyes when what you see is a flattened image of their eyes fixed on some point other than your eyes—a function of how the lens on their device channels their attempt to make eye contact? Or does the fact that you can whisper and still be heard, see your own face transforming as you speak, see the pores of someone else's skin as they respond, etc., carry a miraculous sense of intimacy? Have you tried reversing your image to see yourself as everyone else normally sees you? This experience of reversal is disturbing for everyone with whom I discuss it.

I can only imagine the struggles of elementary school teachers to communicate with their students and parents via technology. But I do know intimately the challenges for university professors thinking about if or how to require or simply beg our students to turn on their cameras so we can *see* them, reflect on their embodied reactions, and attune our presentations to signs of comprehension in their eyes. When things are going well—that is, when I feel I am most virtually "in touch" with my students—there is something so eye-centric about it, and yet it feels larger than that—like the material flesh made mystical. By contrast, when things are not going well, I focus on the gaping cavern of my mouth, and how ugly my teeth and lips look so up close and personal. Yet I must not turn off my camera because that would be to hide in fear.

I turn now to two case studies from my experience of remote teaching in the age of COVID-19. First, I developed and taught a mini course called "Semiotics of Planetary

Health and Justice" in the fall. This was a 1.5 credit class: I was aware that most students had registered for it mid-semester because they were overwhelmed by COVID-related pressures and had gotten behind and withdrawn from some other course. Coming from diverse disciplines, backgrounds, and political commitments, the students shared a vague sense that the course might have something to do with the environment and/or health; most had little to no familiarity with semiotics or anthropology.

In a mere seven weeks, I tried to get them to help think through the ideas that had been bubbling up in me over the past twenty months like the viral variants that have been threatening human forms of social organization as we know it, like the archetypal fruiting bodies of the mycelial connections keeping our carbon-sequestering forests alive, and like the Occupy, Me Too, Black Lives Matter, and climate change protests erupting out of the human bonds of solidarity that reject injustice. Although none of the students were willing (and I did not force them) to turn on their cameras, the skin/screen duality spoke to me viscerally about what forms of human "good" might yet emerge out of this ruinous chaos.

The questions I posed in this course sought to make visceral for my invisible students how biological viruses behave like signs, flowing within and across bodies (both human and otherwise), traversing the fragile membrane that separates the biological "self" from all that is "out there." We are all just assemblages of teeming organisms held together by networks of filaments, many of which are vulnerable to this zoonotic virus, whereas screens are the barriers constructed by humans to both mark our need for privacy and mediate our need to connect. Screens, now made from planet-destroying petrochemicals and heavy metals, provide us with the means to imagine community (diverse, equitable, inclusive) in the midst of destruction.

The second course that I taught remotely was "Language, Food, and Society" in the spring. Before beginning, I worried: How could I (inter)actively engage students in the multisensorial potentialities of food when I could not even make them look at each other, much less smell, taste, or feel each other's food? How would I make them understand the role played by food in environmental destruction and social injustice if they could not do in-person research at factory farms or in food deserts, and then gather in class to discuss their fieldwork afterward? How would they be inspired to engage in food activism if they could barely leave home, much less break bread with others or put their hands in the soil?

Fortunately, two things happened. COVID began to abate in North America. This meant that my students were able to explore the contexts of food production and consumption beyond the confines of their socially isolated spaces, such as by visiting the sustainable student farm on campus. But even before this, the pure joy of food (for those privileged enough to have enough) elicited a remarkable screen-piercing interplay for all of us.

I taught my first class five days after catching Omicron. I was a mess, hacking and feverish. Yet somehow the adrenaline-driven desire to share by Zoom the acorn bread my daughter and I had cooked created a more intimately interactive class than I have ever experienced. Most students turned their cameras on, partly because I asked, but also because they simply felt the need to "be there." The conviviality they already associated with food pulled them into greater connection. This energy continued unabated throughout the semester, and we shared a potluck *in person* on the final day of class. It felt palpable that all of us, vegans and spam-eaters alike, immigrant children with roots in India and Ghana, Iran and Israel, Colombia, the Philippines, and

Ecuador, felt the potential to forge new forms of engagement and balance by foraging, cooking, and eating together. It was a sense-opening experience at all levels, intermingling skin and screen in ways that I would never have imagined possible prior to this two-year period of separation.

Skin and Screen: Signifying a Change of Times

L. AMEDE OBIORA

Among the Igbo of southeastern Nigeria, which is my natal group, *ahu* is the word for skin. However, in my mother tongue, this word has a broader meaning that touches on the essence of skin as a covering for life and being. For example, whereas *ahu adigh mu* means "I am not well," *ahu n'agbakasi mu* indicates that "I am irritable." This resonates with Stacy Klein's discussion of the derivation of the term "skin" from both "animal hide" and "to peel." It reinforces my perception that a key takeaway of sheltering in place to mitigate the impact of COVID-19 is the potential of screen time as a type of "healing touch," to borrow Ellen Ledoux's phrase.

From the perspective of the feminist critique of the objectification of women's bodies, the attenuation, if not redundance, of the social pressure that many women feel to cake up their faces in all sorts of makeup has been remarkable. For instance, it makes little sense to apply a lipstick and then cover up with a mask, especially given that the concealed lipstick ends up soiling the mask.[5] Even more compelling is the potential of the seemingly harsh reality of screen time to "skin," peel, or flay cultural inhibitions that ordinarily regulate our interactions.[6]

To elaborate on this point, I harken again to my native worldview. Masking forces us to look into each other's eyes. For me, this tends to spur empathy in a way that throws into sharp relief the wisdom of the Igbo word for love, which is *ifu n'anya*. This word literally translates to "I see you in my eyes." Some may construe this as analogous to understandings that foreground the eye as the window to the soul, but I find it more evocative of the golden rule, which is an ethical principle that enjoins a person to behave toward others as they would have others behave toward them. COVID-19 brought home the urgency for the world community to come to terms with the fact that adhering to this ethical principle is not sheer benevolence but studied self-preservation.

On November 18, 2022, I was in Lagos, Nigeria. I had two important Zoom meetings that had been scheduled amply in advance. Prior to the meetings, I had been privileged to enjoy uninterrupted power supply through solar-cum-inverter mechanisms that translated into largely glitch-free Zoom connections. But on this fateful day the Wi-Fi chose to fail altogether. I spent hours on the phone with the service provider trying to troubleshoot the problem, to no avail. It dawned on me that this disappointment, which was an exception for me, was the norm for most of my people.

Some across the world are apt to plead compassion fatigue when it comes to Nigeria's development challenges, which parallel the realities of many other nations in the Global South. Yet pandemic mitigation measures have dramatized the absurdities of the digital divide. Even before the outbreak of COVID-19, internal displacements from terrorist extremism and violence in Nigeria demonstrated the basic importance of distance learning. While it is not a magic bullet, there is a growing consensus that educational technology can be harnessed to empower teachers, students, parents, and communities to navigate distance learning (Hawkins et al. 2020). However, distance learning online on mobile phones or computers, and offline using TV, radio, USB keys, and mimeographs, requires compatible ambience, power supply, technology, connectivity, literacy, and skills that remain beyond the means of many.[7]

Assessing the impact of COVID-19 on Nigeria's education system, which was previously stretched and riddled with stark gender inequalities, the Malala Fund (2020) reports that distance learning programs reached only 10 percent of girls via television, 18 percent via radio, and 2 percent via mobile phone. Girls had less intra-household learning support than boys; one-quarter of girls got zero help with distance learning and 61 percent of fathers discouraged their daughters from using the internet. Students with smartphone access lacked the data to connect to others online. Internet services had severe interruptions and electricity shortages impaired available learning tools. Offline take-home materials were often unavailable (Malala Fund 2020).[8]

As bad as these statistics are, the digital divide is not a standalone phenomenon; it reflects broader inequities.[9] The World Bank (2021) estimates that the pandemic pushed up to 40 million people into extreme poverty on the African continent, reversing modest gains that were made in reducing the poverty gap and compounding the risk poverty poses for the future of pandemics. Stressing that success in controlling the virus in Africa is in the interest of the whole world, because no one will be safe if the virus finds sanctuary anywhere, the United Nations secretary-general, António Guterres, underscored the exigent need for the global community to show solidarity with Africa to improve political will, individual and collective commitment, and resource allocation to address Africa's vulnerabilities (United Nations 2020).

The gulf between the rhetoric of global cooperation and the rational allocation of vaccine supplies also spotlights epic inequities. Vaccine nationalism and apartheid explain Africa's persistent trailing of the rest of the world that resulted in the vaccination of a scant 11 percent of its population (WHO Africa 2022). In a speech on November 29, 2021, the director-general of the World Health Organization noted that distortions in the global vaccine supply chain led to 80 percent of vaccines going to wealthier G20 countries. Low-income countries, mainly in Africa, received just 0.6 percent of vaccines (Ghebreyesus 2021). If the most powerful weapon to curb the emergence of new variants is the public health measure of vaccination, the fact that Omicron spread exponentially in the West demonstrates the inherent self-interest of expediting the deployment of vaccines and the impetus for efforts to redouble the golden rule as an avatar of reciprocity.

Lessons from COVID-19 underscore the vital need to bolster preparedness to prevent future pandemics while spurning the temptation to succumb to ideological and material prejudices that arbitrarily stratify, devalue, and penalize skin color and difference. Indeed, while the world was observing cautionary lockdown measures in the interest of public health, the viral streaming of the egregious lynching of George Floyd in the United States on May 25, 2020, jarred the selectively amnesic global consciousness awake to the magnitude of wanton, routinized violence against Black bodies due to the viral contagion of racism. Floyd's public execution by a uniformed state operative galvanized global protests in solidarity with the Black Lives Matter movement to force a meaningful reckoning with the perversions of racism as a standard staple across the globe. More than fifty municipalities in the United States passed legislation or formally declared that racism is a public health crisis. Some counties went further in declaring racism a real pandemic that deserves to be addressed from a comprehensive perspective.[10]

A member of the U.S. House of Representatives, Ayanna Pressley (D-Mass.), introduced the Anti-Racism in Public

Health Act, a bill that formally identifies systemic racism as a public health crisis in the United States (Bellware 2020). By the same token, employees of the Centers for Disease Control (CDC) called on the agency to declare that the deadly racism that has been raging in the United States for centuries is a public health crisis (*Baltimore Sun*, 2020). For their part, professional associations like the American Medical Association, American Academy of Pediatrics, and American Association of Public Health each issued public statements decrying the system of racism that structures opportunity and assigns value arbitrarily and saps the strength of society through the waste of human resources. Others logically affirm that insofar as health inequities are predetermined by the systematic denial of access to resources, structural racism is a social determinant of health (Lincoln 2020).

The impact of the pandemic on health, economies, safety, human rights, and humanitarian assistance highlights the importance of working in solidarity with disadvantaged communities nationally and globally to close gaps in equity in order to advance the security of health as a global public good. The coronavirus pandemic has revealed the dangers of narrow understandings of self-interest, as well as the interdependence of humanity's oneness, or figurative "skin." No country will be able to face this pandemic alone because, as the truism says, "there is no you without me."

Acknowledgments

We thank the seminar participants who were unable to collaborate on this piece yet contributed their inspiration and supportive reflections during our weekly meetings throughout the academic year. We also wish to gratefully acknowledge the contributions, encouragement, and editing skills of our weekly seminar leader, Sarah Tobias—really our wizard behind the screen. Of course, any flaws that remain are our own.

Notes

1. As Holsinger (2015) points out, parchment is not a relic of the past but is still used for special occasions today. For example, English law still mandates that official copies of Acts of Parliament should be printed and preserved on animal skin.
2. For an excellent discussion of the ethical implications of using animals for book production, see Holsinger 2009.
3. *The Wanderer* appears in The Exeter Book (Exeter Cathedral Library MS 3501), one of the four major poetic codices that survive from early medieval England. The manuscript dates from the 960s or 970s, although it is likely that at least some of its contents were circulating prior to the tenth century. *The Wanderer* is a modern title and is not provided in the manuscript itself. For the quotation, see Treharne 2000, 45.
4. Scholars such as Carolyn Dinshaw (1989) have explored the violent and highly gendered implications of close reading. Dinshaw argues that medieval exegesis (the art of interpreting any text, but especially Scripture) characterizes writing and reading as masculine activities performed on a feminized text.
5. Although the lockdown affected businesses across the board, it may be insightful to contrast the pre-pandemic revenue generated from lipstick sales to production and sales at the height of the pandemic.
6. Ellen wrote in the margins of my draft (11/30/21): "I wonder a little bit about this notion that makeup is always oppressive in nature. For example, many gender non-conforming folks have expressed that using makeup has been a very liberatory experience for them (O'Grady 2021). Some women, too, find it a means of artistic expression—or would you consider them to have internalized beauty standards to such a degree that they have

made a 'virtue of necessity'?" To which I responded: "I appreciate your reminder that women are not a monolith—a practice that some may embrace innocuously as empowering may be spurned by others as torture. But my observation here is broader than the ideological critique of makeup as oppressive. Instead, I am probing the impracticality and dissonance of the practice manifest under COVID-19."

7. Human Rights Watch (2020) found children in Africa learned less through distance education due to limited access to technologies, digital illiteracy, intergenerational educational gaps, and living conditions like rural residence, extreme poverty, and insecurity. One interviewee insisted digital learning was a false option where not even a lamp to study exists, let alone electricity. A Nigerian father without a computer said his three children who joined online classes on his phone were unable to view lesson videos. See also Olatunji et al. 2018.

8. Emphasizing the promise of Africa's youth, the UN secretary-general urged African countries to increase digitalization to adapt to the realities of the pandemic. He stressed the need to strengthen internet infrastructure and increase access to technology for education, while at the same time exploring mass media alternatives, especially radio and mobile telecommunication, to expand remote learning platforms. See United Nations 2020.

9. Kathleen wrote in the margins of my draft: "Thank you for this call to arms. After COP26 [the 2021 UN Climate Conference] and the Omicron variant, we need to be taking heed and finding a way to both listen and act on all fronts, from medical and environmental to economic and educational."

10. The New York City Health Commissioner finds that epidemics emerge along the fissures of society, reflecting not only biology but more importantly patterns of marginalization, exclusion, and discrimination related to race, gender, sexuality, class, and more. Citing disparate health inequities, she reports that in New York City, "premature mortality—that's death before the age of 65—is

50 percent higher for black men than white [men]. A black woman in 2012 faced more than 10 times the risk of dying related to childbirth as a white woman . . . and a black baby . . . faces nearly three times the risk of death in its first year of life compared to a white baby" (Bassett 2015). See also Farmer 1996 and 2004.

References

Anthropology News. 2021. "Care" issue, 62, no. 3 (May–June). https://www.anthropology-news.org/issue/care/.

Baltimore Sun. 2020. "CDC Employees Take On Another Pandemic: Racism." July 20, 2020. https://www.baltimoresun.com/opinion/editorial/bs-ed-0720-cdc-diversity-pandemic-20200720-pqnzwn6w3vax7j2fh37cijqreq-story.html.

Bassett, Mary. 2015. "Why Your Doctor Should Care about Social Justice." Filmed November 2015 at TEDMED. Video, 13:39. https://www.ted.com/talks/mary_bassett_why_your_doctor_should_care_about_social_justice.

Beaubien, Jason. 2021. "Peru Has the World's Highest COVID Death Rate. Here's Why." *NPR*, November 27, 2021. https://www.npr.org/sections/goatsandsoda/2021/11/27/1057387896/peru-has-the-worlds-highest-covid-death-rate-heres-why.

Bellware, Kim. 2020. "Calls to Declare Racism a Public Health Crisis Grow Louder amid Pandemic, Police Brutality." *Washington Post*, September 25, 2020. https://www.washingtonpost.com/nation/2020/09/15/racism-public-health-crisis/.

Best, Stephen, and Sharon Marcus. 2009. "Surface Reading: An Introduction." *Representations* 108, no. 1 (Fall): 1–21.

Dinshaw, Carolyn. 1989. *Chaucer's Sexual Poetics*. Madison: University of Wisconsin Press.

Doyle, Nora. 2018. *Maternal Bodies: Redefining Motherhood in Early America*. Chapel Hill: University of North Carolina Press.

Farmer, Paul. 1996. "On Suffering and Structural Violence: A View from Below." *Daedalus* 125, no. 1 (Winter): 251–283.

———. 2004. "An Anthropology of Structural Violence." *Current Anthropology* 45 (3): 305–325. https://doi.org/10.1086/382250.

Ghebreyesus, Tedros Adhanom. 2021. "WHO Director-General's Opening Remarks at the Stakeholder Engagement Event." World Health Organization, December 6, 2021. https://www .who.int/director-general/speeches/detail/who-director-generals -opening-remarks-progress-made-so-far-on-implementing-the -partnerships-for-vaccine-manufacturing-in-africa.

Haraway, Donna Jeanne. 2016. *Staying With the Trouble: Making Kin in the Chthulucene*. Durham, NC: Duke University Press.

Hawkins, Robert, Michael Trucano, Cristóbal Cobo, Alex Twinomugisha, and Iñaki Sánchez Ciarrusta. 2020. *Reimagining Human Connections: Technology and Innovation in Education at the World Bank*. Washington, DC: World Bank. https://documents1 .worldbank.org/curated/en/829491606860379513/pdf/Reimagining -Human-Connections-Technology-and-Innovation-in-Education -at-the-World-Bank.pdf.

Holsinger, Bruce. 2009. "Of Pigs and Parchment: Medieval Studies and the Coming of the Animal." *PMLA* 124, no. 2 (March): 616–623.

———. 2015. "Written on Beasts." *New York Review of Books*, November 25, 2015.

Horsley, Scott. 2020. "'Something Has to Give': Latinas Leaving Workforce at Faster Rate Than Other Groups." *NPR*, October 27, 2020. https://www.npr.org/2020/10/27/927793195 /something-has-to-give-latinas-leaving-workforce-at-faster-rate -than-other-groups.

Human Rights Watch. 2020. "Impact of COVID-19 on Children's Education in Africa. 35th Ordinary Session." August 26, 2020. https://www.hrw.org/news/2020/08/26/impact-covid-19 -childrens-education-africa.

Kirana, Evie, and Francesca Tripodi. 2020. "Sexual Relationships during the Lockdown: Adjusting Sexual Counselling and Therapy to the Restriction of Quarantine." *ESSM—European Society for*

Sexual Medicine 43 (August): 3–8. https://www.essm.org/wp
-content/uploads/publications/essm-today/ESSM2020
_Newsletter_August.pdf.

Lincoln, Karen D. 2020. "Racism Is the Most Significant Underlying Condition in the COVID-19 Pandemic." Poynter Institute,
October 8, 2020. https://www.poynter.org/reporting-editing
/2020/racism-is-the-most-significant-underlying-condition-in
-the-covid-19-pandemic/.

Love, Heather. 2010. "Close but Not Deep: Literary Ethics and the
Descriptive Turn." *New Literary History* 41, no. 2 (Spring):
371–391.

Lowe, Lisa. 2015. *The Intimacies of Four Continents*. Durham: Duke
University Press.

Malala Fund. 2020. *Girls' Education and COVID-19 in Nigeria*.
Washington, DC: Malala Fund. https://malala.org/newsroom
/girls-education-and-covid-19-in-nigeria.

Melville, Herman. (1851) 2001. *Moby-Dick; or, The Whale*. Reprint,
New York: Penguin Books.

Msomi, Nokukhanya, Richard Lessells, Koleka Mlisana, and Tulio
de Oliveira. 2021. "Africa: Tackle HIV and COVID-19
Together." *Nature*, December 1, 2021. https://www.nature.com
/articles/d41586-021-03546-8.

O'Grady, Megan. 2021. "Makeup Is for Everyone." *New York Times*,
May 10, 2021. https://www.nytimes.com/2021/05/10/t-magazine
/men-makeup-gender-norms.html.

Olatunji, Obafemi, Stephen Akinlabi, Ajayi Oluseyi, Abiodun
Abioye, Felix Ishola, Mashinini Peter, and Nkosinathi Madush-
ele. 2018. "Electric Power Crisis in Nigeria: A Strategic Call for
Change of Focus to Renewable Sources." *IOP Conference Series:
Materials Science and Engineering* 413 (July):012053. https://doi
.org/10.1088/1757-899X/413/1/012053.

O'Neill, Eugene. 1926. *The Great God Brown*. In *The Great God
Brown, The Fountain, The Moon of the Caribbees, and Other Plays*,
8–98. New York: Boni & Liveright.

Oxford English Dictionary Online. n.d.a. "Screen, Noun." Accessed October 26, 2022. https://www.oed.com/view/Entry/173439.

Oxford English Dictionary Online. n.d.b. "Skin, Noun." Accessed October 26, 2022. https://www.oed.com/view/Entry/180922.

Patchett, Ann. 2009. "The Triumph of the Readers." *Wall Street Journal*, January 17, 2009. https://www.wsj.com/articles /SB123214794600191819.

Ranji, Usha, Brittni Frederiksen, Alina Salganicoff, and Michelle Long. 2021. "Women, Work, and Family during COVID-19: Findings from the KFF Women's Health Survey." Kaiser Family Foundation, March 22, 2021. https://www.kff.org/womens -health-policy/issue-brief/women-work-and-family-during -covid-19-findings-from-the-kff-womens-health-survey/.

Treharne, Elaine, ed. 2000. *The Wanderer*. In *Old and Middle English: An Anthology*, 42–47. Oxford: Wiley-Blackwell.

Tsing, Anna Lowenhaupt, Heather Anne Swanson, Elaine Gan, and Nils Bubandt, eds. 2017. *Arts of Living on a Damaged Planet: Ghosts and Monsters of the Anthropocene*. Minneapolis: University of Minnesota Press.

United Nations. 2020. *Policy Brief: Impact of COVID-19 in Africa*. May 20, 2020. https://www.un.org/sites/un2.un.org/files/2020/05 /sg_policy_brief_on_covid-19_impact_on_africa_may_2020.pdf.

Wollstonecraft, Mary. 2003. *The Collected Letters of Mary Wollstonecraft*. Edited by Janet Todd. New York: Columbia University Press.

World Bank. 2021. "World Bank's Response to COVID-19 (Coronavirus) in Africa." April 8, 2021. https://www.worldbank .org/en/news/factsheet/2020/06/02/world-banks-response-to -covid-19-coronavirus-in-africa.

World Health Organization African Region (WHO Africa). 2022. "Africa on Track to Control COVID-19 Pandemic in 2022." February 10, 2022. https://www.afro.who.int/news/africa-track -control-covid-19-pandemic-2022.

Acknowledgments

Public Catastrophes, Private Losses is the third volume in the Institute for Research on Women's series *The Feminist Bookshelf: Ideas for the 21st Century*, which showcases innovative feminist scholarship that was first presented, or had its origins in, the annual IRW Distinguished Lecture Series or the institute's seminar. We thank Rutgers University Press's Editorial Director, Kimberly Guinta, for nurturing our series and this book. This volume originates from IRW's programming in the 2018–2019 academic year, when our annual theme was "Public Catastrophes, Private Losses." We thank all the participants in our programming that year, and also thank the seminar fellows from our "Knowing Bodies" cohort, who helped inspire chapter 5 in this volume, especially Kathleen C. Riley, who was the driving force behind "Skin and Screen."

We thank the Rutgers School of Arts and Sciences, especially Dean of Humanities Rebecca Walkowitz and former Dean Michelle Stephens, for supporting IRW's programming. We thank current IRW Director and former IRW Executive Committee member Chie Ikeya. We also thank current and recent IRW Executive Committee members: Tyler Carson, Alexandra Chang, Sylvia Chan-Malik, Asenath Dande, Kayo Denda, Leah DeVun, Anette Freytag, Suzanne Kim, Suzy Kim, Preetha Mani, Rebecca Mark, Sara

Perryman, Priscilla Pinto-Ferreira, Nancy Rao, Kyla Schuller, Ethel Brooks, Joanie Mazelis, and Cat Fitzpatrick. We are greatly indebted to our former administrative assistant, Andrea Zerpa, who helped with the logistics of our 2018–2019 programming. In addition, we thank IRW's current administrative assistant Alexandra Singh, and our former work-study student and *Chicago Manual of Style* expert, Moazima Ahmad.

Arlene thanks Sarah Tobias for her smarts and dedication, and for making IRW such an amazing feminist space. She also thanks the department of sociology at Rutgers, Cynthia Chris, and Stormy Daniels.

Sarah thanks Arlene Stein for her inspirational leadership, as well as her generosity, good humor, and impeccable editorial skills. She thanks Chie Ikeya and the beautiful intellectual community that finds its home at IRW. She also thanks Beth, Talila, and everyone who has supported her while she edited this volume.

Notes on Contributors

MICHELLE COMMANDER is a museum administrator, writer, curator, and scholar of slavery and memory, Black geographies, and the speculative arts. Her books include *Afro-Atlantic Flight: Speculative Returns and the Black Fantastic* and *Avidly Reads: Passages*. She is the editor of the anthology *Unsung: Unheralded Narratives of American Slavery & Abolition*. Commander recently served as the consulting curator of *Before Yesterday We Could Fly: An Afrofuturist Period Room* at the Metropolitan Museum of Art. She is an elected member of the American Antiquarian Society.

BASULI DEB is a professorial research associate at the SOAS School of Law, Gender and Media in London. She is currently engaged with Columbia Law School's Center for Contemporary Critical Thought, and has been a visiting scholar at Columbia's Institute for Comparative Literature & Society as well as Columbia's Institute for the Study of Human Rights. She is the author of *Transnational Feminist Perspectives on Terror in Literature and Culture* and co-editor of *Indigenous Feminisms Across the World* and *Transnational Inquiries*. Deb is a steering committee member of the international editorial collective Federation for Feminist Publishing Futures. She is a former global scholar at the Institute for Research on Women at Rutgers University, where she co-founded the International Working Group on Dalit and Adivasi Studies.

MARISA J. FUENTES is associate professor of history and women's, gender, and sexuality studies and Presidential Term Chair in African American History, 2017–2026 at Rutgers University–New Brunswick. She is the author of *Dispossessed Lives: Enslaved Women, Violence, and the Archive*, which won the Letitia Woods Brown Book Prize from the Association of Black Women Historians, the Barbara T. Christian Best Humanities Book Prize, and the Berkshire Conference of Women Historians First Book Prize. *Dispossessed Lives* illuminates the lives of enslaved women in eighteenth-century Bridgetown, Barbados. The book interrogates the archive and its historical production to challenge the methods and categories by which historians have analyzed slavery in the Atlantic World and to engage with larger questions of violence, agency, and gender.

MARCIA M. GALLO is professor emerita of history at the University of Nevada, Las Vegas. Her books include the prize-winning *Different Daughters: A History of the Daughters of Bilitis and the Rise of the Lesbian Rights Movement* and *"No One Helped": Kitty Genovese, New York City, and the Myth of Urban Apathy*, which won both the 2015 Lambda Literary Award for LGBT Nonfiction and the 2015 Publishing Triangle Judy Grahn Award for Lesbian Nonfiction. It was also a finalist for the 2015 USA Book News Best Book Awards for Gay & Lesbian Nonfiction. Gallo has contributed essays and book chapters exploring post–World War II feminism, progressive queer politics, and oral history methodology to journals as well as edited collections.

SMRUTHI BALA KANNAN is a postdoctoral scholar at the University of Chicago. Her research focuses on children's lived experiences and discourses of sustainability, and health. In 2020–2021 she was a seminar fellow at the Institute for Research on Women at Rutgers University. She has a PhD in Childhood Studies from Rutgers University–Camden.

NAOMI KLEIN is an award-winning journalist and *New York Times* bestselling author. She is a columnist for *The Guardian*. In 2018 she was named the inaugural Gloria Steinem Endowed Chair at Rutgers University and is now an honorary professor of media and climate at Rutgers University. In September 2021 she joined the University of British Columbia as professor of climate justice and co-director of the Centre for Climate Justice.

STACY S. KLEIN is an associate professor of English at Rutgers University–New Brunswick, where she also serves as graduate faculty in the Women's, Gender, and Sexuality Studies Department. She is the author of *Ruling Women: Queenship and Gender in Anglo-Saxon Literature*, and has co-edited several interdisciplinary volumes, including *The Maritime World of the Anglo-Saxons*, with William Schipper and Shannon Lewis-Simpson, and *Anglo-Saxon England and the Visual Imagination*, with John Niles and Jonathan Wilcox. Klein has published numerous articles on Old English language and literature, gender and the history of sexuality, premodern disability, birds, environmental humanism, hagiography, and aesthetics. She is currently completing a monograph entitled *The Militancy of Gender and the Making of Sexual Difference in Early English Literature, ca. 700–1100 AD*.

ELLEN MALENAS LEDOUX is an associate professor of English at Rutgers University–Camden. She specializes in Romantic and Gothic literature. Her book *Social Reform in Gothic*

Writing: Fantastic Forms of Change, 1764–1834 examines the relationship between Gothic texts and social reform in transatlantic writers of the Revolutionary era. Her book *Laboring Mothers: Reproducing Women and Work in the Eighteenth Century* focuses on the material challenges of motherhood faced by women working in the late eighteenth and early nineteenth centuries as represented in literature, art, and popular culture.

L. AMEDE OBIORA served as the minister of mines and steel development for the Federal Republic of Nigeria and is currently a professor of law at the University of Arizona. A former manager of the World Bank Gender and Law Program, she was a Genest Global Faculty member at York University in Toronto, the Gladstein Visiting Professor of Human Rights at the University of Connecticut, and a Coca Cola World Fund Visiting Faculty member at Yale University. She is the recipient of prestigious fellowships from the Institute for Advanced Study at Princeton, the Center for Advanced Study in the Behavioral Sciences at Stanford, the Rockefeller Foundation Bellagio Study Center, and the Djerassi Resident Artist Program.

KATHLEEN C. RILEY is a cultural and linguistic anthropologist who has conducted fieldwork in the Marquesas Islands, Vermont, France, Montreal, and New York City. Her research focuses on the relationship between language ideologies and language socialization, language shift, and culturally constructed social identities (indigeneity, ethnicity, class, gender, and sexuality). She is co-author, with Amy Paugh, of *Food and Language: Discourses and Foodways across Cultures*. She is visiting assistant research professor in the Anthropology Department at Rutgers University–New Brunswick.

CHRISTINA SHARPE is a writer, professor, and Tier 1 Canada Research Chair in Black studies in the humanities at York University. She is the author of *In the Wake: On Blackness and Being*, which was named by both *The Guardian* and *The Walrus* as one of the best books of 2016 and was a nonfiction finalist for the Hurston/Wright Legacy Award. She is also the author of *Monstrous Intimacies: Making Post-Slavery Subjects* and *Ordinary Notes*, which won multiple awards and was a finalist for the National Book Award in Nonfiction and the National Book Critics Circle Award in Nonfiction.

ARLENE STEIN is Distinguished Professor of Sociology and serves on the graduate faculty of the Women's, Gender, and Sexuality Studies Department at Rutgers University. She was the director of the Institute for Research on Women from 2016 to 2022. Her research focuses on the intersections of gender, sexuality, culture, and politics. Her most recent book is *Unbound: Transgender Men and the Transformation of Identity*. She is also the author of *Reluctant Witnesses: Survivors, their Children, and the Rise of Holocaust Consciousness*, which looks at how feminism and therapeutic culture facilitated the telling of Holocaust stories in the United States.

SARAH TOBIAS is executive director of the Institute for Research on Women at Rutgers University, where she also serves as affiliate faculty in the Women's, Gender, and Sexuality Studies Department. She is co-author of *Policy Issues Affecting Lesbian, Gay, Bisexual, and Transgender Families*, and co-editor of *Trans Studies: The Challenge to Hetero/Homo Normativities*, which won the 2017 Sylvia Rivera Award for Best Book in Transgender Studies from the City University of New York's Center for Lesbian and Gay Studies. With Arlene Stein, she is series editor of *The Feminist Bookshelf: Ideas for the 21st Century*. Books in the series include

The Perils of Populism and *Feeling Democracy: Emotional Politics in the New Millennium*.

CARMEN VÁZQUEZ was an activist and organizer with a long history of working to foster social and racial justice in the women's and LGBTQ movements. Her activist career began in San Francisco during the 1970s when she co-founded the Women's Building. She became the executive director of the National Network for Immigrant and Refugee Rights and then the coordinator of lesbian and gay health services for the San Francisco Department of Public Health. Moving to New York City in the 1990s, she worked as director of public policy for the LGBT Community Center in 1994–2003, as deputy director for Empire State Pride Agenda in 2003–2007, and as coordinator of the LGBT Health and Human Services Unit of the AIDS Institute, New York Department of Health from 2008 to her passing in 2021. She was awarded an honorary law degree from the City University of New York School of Law in 2005.

BELA AUGUST WALKER is an adjunct professor of law at Rutgers Law School and has taught law at Roger Williams University School of Law, Fordham University, and the City University of New York. They have been published in the *University of Texas Law Review*, the *DePaul Law Review*, and the *Columbia Law Review*, among others. Professor Walker has clerked for the Honorable Sidney R. Thomas of the U.S. Court of Appeals for the Ninth Circuit and for the Honorable Robert P. Patterson of the U.S. District Court for the Southern District of New York. They also served as staff attorney at the Public Interest Law Center of Philadelphia.

JENNIFER FLYNN WALKER is the co-chief of campaigns at the Center for Popular Democracy in Brooklyn, New York, where she previously served as director of mobilization and advocacy. She is the co-founder and former executive director of VOCAL-NY (previously NYC AIDS Housing Network), where she organized around welfare rights, homelessness, drug user rights, and immigration, winning campaigns that resulted in a progressive right to housing legislation and over $30 million in funding to build housing. Prior to VOCAL-NY, she served as the managing director of Health GAP (Global Access Project), an international AIDS advocacy organization that led campaigns resulting in over $50 billion for AIDS treatment.

Index

abandonment: organized, 38; register of, 17, 52, 61
Abrams, Donald, 119
Achtenberg, Roberta, 133
ACLU, 108, 113, 114, 137
ACT UP, 21n2, 105, 126
adoption, 77, 83, 85
Adoption and Safe Families Act (1997), 17, 77, 87, 88n6
Africa: and climate change, 9; and COVID-19 pandemic, 18, 158–159, 163–166; and HIV/AIDS, 158; and online education, 164–165, 169nn7–8; and poverty, 165; and vaccine supplies, 158, 159, 165–166
Agatha (enslaved woman), 54
AIDS. *See* HIV/AIDS
AIDS Memorial Quilt, 14, 128, 129
air quality, wildfire smoke affecting, 1
Albrecht, Glenn, 7, 31–32
Aldarondo, Celia, 20
Amazon rainforest fires, 6
American Public Health Association, 78
Andriote, John-Manuel, 122
Angélique, Marie-Joseph, 54, 56
animal skin, 146–147, 163, 168nn1–2; ethical issues in use of, 147, 168n2
Anthropocene disorder, 7–8

anti-Black racism, 4, 10–13. *See also* racism
Anti-Racism in Public Health Act, 166–167
Apuzzo, Ginny, 128
Ar'n't I a Woman? (Deborah Gray White), 60
art: as green job, 37, 38; *trompe l'oeil* technique in, 113
Asian American and Pacific Islander communities: and COVID-19, 106; and children in foster care, 76; and HIV/AIDS, 114, 123
Ault, Steve, 128
Australia, bushfires in, 6
AZT therapy in HIV/AIDS, 120–121

Barbados, history of enslaved Black women in, 17, 43–45, 47, 51, 54
Barbados Council, 43, 44–45
Baum, Dan, 71
Bay Area Lawyers for Individual Freedom, 114
Bay Area Reporter, 114, 127
Beaubien, Jason, 155
Beck, Charlie, 56
Beloved (Toni Morrison), 50

COVID-19 pandemic (cont.)
domestic violence during, 5; drug
overdose deaths during, 67;
education during (*see* education
during COVID-19 pandemic);
employment during, 13, 105, 117,
152–155; essential workers in, 13,
105, 117; family stress during, 84;
government response to, 18, 105,
106, 109, 112, 116, 117, 127; HIV/
AIDS onset compared to, 16, 18,
104–140; initial misinformation
and confusion about, 106–107,
109, 130; isolation and quarantine
during, 107, 109, 116–117, 122, 123,
130; and life expectancy trends
in U.S., 86; long COVID, 5;
makeup and lipstick use during,
163, 168–169nn5–6; mask use
during, 123, 124, 130, 163; number
of deaths from, 19, 105, 109, 114,
122, 124, 127, 130, 136, 155;
Omicron variant in, 158–159, 162,
166; personal losses in, 16, 126,
136–139; pre-existing inequalities
affecting impact of, 13, 21n1, 106,
118; skin, screen, and touch in,
18–19, 142–170; social distancing
in, 105, 106, 124, 155; social
structuring of worth in, 13;
substance abuse treatment
during, 81–82; vaccines in, 107,
155, 158, 159, 165–166; women in,
117, 118, 150, 152, 153–155
Craps, Stef, 7, 8
Crèvecoeur, Jean de, 53
criminalization of drug use, 68–69,
86; compared to public health
approach, 79–81; in War on
Drugs, 68–69, 72
Cullors, Patrisse, 4
Cunsolo, A., 7
Cuomo, Andrew, 104

custody decisions in child welfare
system, 74, 77–79

daguerreotypes of enslaved
people, 61
Danylevich, Theodora, 11
dating events, online, during
COVID-19 pandemic, 156
death: of African Americans in
police custody, 4, 56; from climate
change, 4, 31, 37; in COVID-19
pandemic, 19, 105, 109, 114, 122,
124, 127, 130, 136, 155; and HIV/
AIDS, 20, 111, 114, 115, 121, 125–126;
in opioid epidemic, 68, 70, 80–81,
83, 87–88n1; from police violence,
11, 13–14, 62; pre-existing
inequalities affecting, 13, 21n1;
during slavery, 43–45, 46, 47, 53,
55–56, 57 134
Deb, Basuli, 16, 19, 156–159
Declaration of Independence (U.S.),
134–135
decriminalization of drug
possession, 80
Delia (enslaved woman), 61
Denny, John, 43
digital divide, 164, 165
Dinshaw, Carolyn, 168n4
disasters: natural, 2, 3, 29–31;
socially produced, 3. *See also*
catastrophes
discrimination, sexual orientation as
basis of, 131
Dispossessed Lives (Marisa Fuentes),
17, 43–48, 51, 52, 53; autobiographical "I" in, 60; epilogue of, 60, 62
domestic abuse and violence, 5, 30,
74, 157
Douglass, Frederick, 55, 135
Dowler, Lorraine, 5–6
Doyle, Nora, 153
drinking water, lead in, 10

Haley, Sarah, 45
Hanging of Angélique, The (Afua
  Cooper), 54
harm reduction programs in
  substance use, 18, 68, 80, 82
Harris, Kamala, 19
Hartman, Saidiya, 12, 42, 43, 44, 48,
  59; *Lose Your Mother,* 58; *Scenes of
  Subjection,* 60; *Wayward Lives,
  Beautiful Experiments,* 52
healing: care work in, 37–38;
  community relationships in, 3;
  touch in, 153–154, 163
health care: in Green New Deal, 36,
  37; in HIV/AIDS, 118, 119–121;
  opioid prescription in, 70, 71,
  72–73; racial bias in, 13, 71, 73; in
  substance abuse treatment, 68, 74,
  81–82; unequal access to, 106, 167;
  universal, 36, 37
health insurance access: and
  COVID-19 vulnerability, 13; in
  HIV diagnosis, 118
H/Esther (enslaved woman), 55
Hichens, Donna, 133
Hines-Brim, Sheila, 56
Hiroshima bombing survivors,
  2–3
Hispanic children in foster care, 76
historical studies on enslaved
  people, 42–63; do no harm
  approach in, 17, 59–60; ethical
  issues in, 17, 47–49, 59–61;
  replication of violence in, 17,
  48–49, 59, 60
HIV/AIDS, 4; activism concerning,
  14, 21–22n2, 108, 128–129, 133; in
  Africa, 158; AZT therapy in,
  120–121; coping with illness in
  others, 121–122; COVID-19
  pandemic compared to onset of,
  16, 18, 104–140; government
  response to, 18, 106, 112, 115, 118,
133; grief and mourning in, 14,
  104–139; initial misinformation
  and confusion about, 106–107,
  110–111, 120, 130; memorial quilt,
  14, 128, 129; national memorial for,
  20; number of deaths from, 20, 111,
  114, 115, 121, 125–126; personal
  losses in, 110, 111–115, 116, 121–123,
  129; pre-existing inequalities
  affecting impact of, 106, 118;
  transmission of, 110, 126, 130
Holocaust, 2
Holsinger, Bruce, 168n1
homelessness: and HIV/AIDS, 112,
  117; and substance abuse disorder,
  79, 80
homeschooling during COVID-19
  pandemic, 150
homesickness, and concerns about
  future in climate change, 32
Hooker, Juliet, 13
hospitalization rate in opioid
  epidemic, 83
housing, and opioid epidemic, 74,
  79, 80, 82
Hudson, Rock, 115
Human Rights Watch, 169n7
Hurricane Harvey, 29, 33
Hurricane Maria, 29, 30–31, 37

Igbo of Nigeria, 19, 163–164
incarceration, for drug offenses,
  68–69, 71, 72, 79; of Black
  Americans, 69, 71, 72, 79;
  compared to public health
  approach, 81; of women, 74,
  88n2
incarceration, and prison labor, 38
India: COVID-19 in, 18; caste
  system of, 157
Indian Child Welfare Act, 75
Indigeneity. *See* Native American
  and Indigenous Peoples

Norman, Pat, 108, 110, 128
nursing home residents, as vulnerable population in climate change, 33

Obama administration, 36
Obiora, L. Amede, 16, 19, 163–167
Ocasio-Cortez, Alexandria, 34, 38, 136
Omicron variant, 158–159, 162, 166
omnicide, 4
O'Neill, Eugene, 148
opioid epidemic, 16, 17–18, 67–88; and child welfare system, 17–18, 69, 82–85, 86–87; criminalization of drug use in, 68–69, 72, 79–81, 86; drug companies in, 70, 86; drug dependence in, 68; harm reduction programs in, 18, 68, 80, 82; hospitalization rate in, 83; iatrogenic addiction in, 73; medication-assisted treatment of substance abuse in, 68, 74, 81–82; overdose deaths in, 68, 70, 80–81, 83, 86, 87–88n1; over-policing in, 68, 69; prescription practices in, 70, 71, 72–73, 81, 86; public health approach to, 18, 67, 71, 79–81, 87; stereotypes on drug users in, 71, 72;
orphan trains, 75
Osberg, Kay, 128
overdose deaths, 68, 70, 80–81, 83, 86, 87–88n1
over-policing in opioid epidemic, 68, 69
OxyContin, 70, 86

Pacific Islander communities: and COVID-19, 106; and National Task Force on AIDS, 123
pain, prescription of opioids for, 73, 86

Pannell, Kraig, 105
parents: addiction treatment in, 82, 84; childcare responsibilities during COVID-19 pandemic, 150, 152, 153–155; and child welfare system, 17–18 (*see also* child welfare system); healing touch of, 153; homeschooling children, 150; separation of children from, 17–18, 67, 69, 75–79, 82–85, 87; of son killed by police, 62
parole population, 11
Patsavas, Alyson, 11
people of color: and child welfare system, 75–76, 78, 86–87; climate change vulnerability, 9; COVID-19 in, 13, 18, 136; and Green New Deal policies, 35; HIV/AIDS in, 18, 20, 21–22n2, 111, 122–123; incarceration for drug offenses, 69, 71, 72, 74, 79; violence against, 3, 12; water pollution and environmental hazards for, 10. *See also* Black Americans; Brown communities
people with disabilities, as vulnerable population in climate change, 33
Perkins, Ben, 4–5
Peru, COVID-19 pandemic in, 155
police: Black Americans killed by, 11, 13–14, 62, 134; Bland death in custody of, 4; Wilson death in custody of, 56
Portugal, drug policies in, 80
poverty: in Africa, 165; COVID-19 vulnerability in, 13, 21n1; and drug addiction, 79
pregnancy, substance use during, 84; and methadone treatment, 74
prescription of opioids, 70, 81, 86; and buprenorphine compared, 81;

Wagner, Peter, 10
wake, multiple definitions of, 50
wake work, 14, 50, 57
Walker, Bela August, 16, 17–18, 67–88
Walker, Jennifer Flynn, 16, 17–18, 67–88
Wanderer, The, 147–148, 168n3
Ward 5B of San Francisco General Hospital, 119–120, 121, 122, 139n1
Ward 86 of San Francisco General Hospital, 119–120, 139n1
Warner, Doug, 108, 112–115, 116, 120–122, 138
War on Drugs, 67–88; people of color as targets of, 72; racism in origin of, 71–72; women impacted by, 69, 72–74
Washington, DC, March on Washington for Lesbian and Gay Rights (1987) in, 128–129
water supply, pollutants in, 10
Wayward Lives, Beautiful Experiments (Saidiya Hartman), 52
wealth inequality, 36, 87
weather events in climate change, 29–31. *See also* climate change
Weheliye, Alexander, 46
Weston, Kath, 114
White, Deborah Gray, 60
whites: in ACT-UP, 21n2; and bias in child welfare system, 78; drug use of, 71, 72, 73; in foster care, 75, 76; HIV/AIDS in, 114, 117, 122; incarceration rate of, 10, 72, 134; privacy rights of, 76; as slave owners, 44, 51, 54–55; violence against Black Americans, 12, 13–14

white supremacy, 85; and child welfare system, 74–79, 88n3; and legacy of slave trade, 47, 50–51, 52; and War on Drugs, 72
wildfires, 1, 6, 29
Williams, Reggie, 108, 122–123
Wilson, Phil, 122
Wilson, Wakiesha, 56
Wintour, Patrick, 6, 7
witnessing by Black Americans, 12
Wofsy, Connie, 119
women: as care workers after trauma, 37; childcare responsibilities of, 150, 152, 153–155; COVID-19 impact in, 117, 118, 150, 152, 153–155; in drug trade, 88n2; drug use and addiction of, 72–74, 84; enslaved, 17, 43–45, 47, 48, 51–56, 134; as essential workers, 117; HIV/AIDS in, 117–118; War on Drugs affecting, 69, 72–74; work-life balance for, 152–153
Women's Building (San Francisco), 110, 119, 133
World Bank, 165
World Health Organization, 166
Wray, Isaac, 44

youth movement on climate change, 32, 34, 35

Zal, Eli, 104
Zoom use during COVID-19 pandemic, 142, 159–160; for dating events, 156; fatigue from, 143, 154; in Nigeria, challenges in, 164; for teaching, 19, 150–151, 152, 160–163